A COLLECTION OF CLASSIC ESSAYS

Including 'Happiness', 'Superstition', 'The Great American Game', and Many More

BY

WILLIAM LYON PHELPS

British Library Cataloguing-in-Publication Data
A catalogue record for this book is available from the
British Library

Contents

William Lyon Phelps

William Lyon Phelps was born on 2nd January 1865, in New Haven, Conneticut, United States.

Phelps earned a B.A. in 1887, writing his thesis on the Idealism of George Berkeley. He then gained an M.A. in 1891 from Yale and his PhD from Harvard in the same year. During his time a Yale, he offered a course in modern novels which brought the university considerable attention both nationally and internationally. This was quite controversial at the time and Phelps was pressured to give up the course, but eventually, due to popular demand, reinstated it outside the official curriculum.

In 1892, Phelps married Annabel Hubbard, sister of childhood friend Frank Hubbard, and the couple moved to the family estate overlooking Lake Huron. Phelps christened it "The House of the Seven Gables", after the Nathanial Hawthorne story of the same name.

He became a very popular figure at Yale but also as an inspirational orator. He went on lecture tours that drew large audiences, speaking on the virtues of modern literature. He also preached regularly at the Huron City Methodist Episcopal Church and attracted such large crowds that the church was remodelled twice in five years to accommodate them.

Phelps published many essays on modern and European literature, including titles such as *Essays on Modern Novelists* (1910), *Some Makers of American Literature* (1923), and *As I Like it* (1923).

After his retirement from Yale in 1933, after 41 years of service, Phelps continued his public speaking, preaching, and writing a newspaper column. He also sat on book selection committees and acted as a judge for the Pulitzer Prize for literature.

His wife, Annabel, died from a stroke in 1939 and Phelps died four years later, in 1943.

AMBITION

What do we really mean when we say of a man, "He is too good for this world?" Do we mean exactly that, do we mean he is so far loftier in character than the average person that he seems almost out of place in a world like this? Don't we rather mean that he lacks human sympathy and understanding, and therefore can be of no real use to anybody?

If you remember the character of Hilda in Hawthorne's novel, *The Marble Faun, you* may remember that she used to be held up as an ideal of the religious life. "Her soul was like a star and dwelt apart." But from the selfish sanctity of its seclusion, no real good resulted; no one was aided or cheered in the struggle of life. No one could confide in her, for she could not even confide in herself. Her nature may have had the purity of an angel, but it lacked the purity of a noble woman. She was no help to sinners; she was their despair. Her purity was like that of one who hesitates to rescue a drowning man, for fear of soiling his clothes.

Hilda gave up the world and worldly pleasure; easily enough, for she abhorred it, and felt ill at ease in society. But though she gave up many things precious to the average person, she had no conception of the meaning of the word *self* denial.

For the true sacrifice, if one wishes to be of real use in this world, consists not in the giving of things, but in giving oneself. If a man's life consists not in the abundance of things which he possesses, so the sacrificial life consists not in the number of luxuries one surrenders, but in the devotion of oneself, in the denial of the will. There is a certain kind of purity which is fundamentally selfish.

This manner of asceticism is not particularly common nowadays, and we need not fear that it will be too generally practiced. I am calling attention to it in order to show that selfishness may take on the mask of purity or of respectability, a selfishness that springs from pure moral motives and a longing for the elevation of character.

But there is another type of respectable selfishness that is far more common, possibly more common in America than in any other country. It is not usually recognised as selfishness, but regarded as one of the greatest-perhaps the greatest of the virtues. It is seen chiefly among earnest and ambitious young men, who assume that life is not a holiday, but a serious affair, a struggle, a strictly competitive race, where if you stop a moment, even for reflexion, you are left behind.

We are bound to respect these men. They have at all events found out half the secret of life. They have set before themselves some goal, in politics, in business, in literature, and they are determined to reach it. They are equally determined to gain the prize by no dishonourable means. Their minds are full of the lessons learned from their predecessors, men who by the sacrifice of temporary pleasures, by the refusal to indulge in recreation or relaxation, have surpassed their competitors and reached the top.

We are constantly told that it is only by intense concentration, by terrific efforts day and night, and by keeping the end constantly in view that one can attain success. Surely these young men are to be admired, surely they are models, examples worthy of emulation?

Well, they are better than criminals, they are better than parasites, they are better than drones. But their driving motive is selfishness. Tennyson wrote The *Palace of Art,* Browning

wrote Paracelsus, because each of these poets knew that his individual danger was not what is usually known as "temptation." They knew that they would never go to hell by the crowded highway of dissipation, for they were above the mere call of the blood. Their danger lay in a high and noble ambition, which has wrecked many first-rate minds.

Modern life tends to encourage this respectable selfishness. The central law of the socalled science of Economics is selfishness. A whole science is built on one foundation-that every man in the world will get all he can for himself. The subject is naturally studied not from an ethical, but from a scientific standpoint. Life is a race.

Now I believe that Efficiency-mere practical success in the world-is as false an ideal as asceticism. If the morality of withdrawal is not good enough, neither is the morality of success. Those deserve the highest admiration and the most profound respect who have actually aided their human brethren, who have left the world better than they found it.

This is by no means a hopeless ideal of character. It is not necessary to crush a tyrant or to organise a revolution or to reconstruct society or to be a professional reformer. There are plenty of professional reformers who have tremendous enthusiasm for humanity and who have never helped an individual. Those who by unselfish lives and consideration for others elevate the tone of the community in which they live and who by their presence make others happier, these are the salt of the earth. Their daily existence is more eloquent than a sermon.

American young men and women in our High Schools and universities are not often face to face with the mystery of life. They have no conception of the amount of suffering in the world. Their own lives are comparatively free from it, in many cases free even from anxiety. These boys and girls are for the most part sensible, alert, quick-witted, and practical;

what I should like to see would be a change in their ideals from mere Success to something nobler. I should like to see them devoting their intelligence and energy to the alleviation of suffering and to the elevation of human thought and life.

If one still believes that the highest happiness and satisfaction come from the attainment of any selfish ambition, no matter how worthy in itself, it is well to remember the significance of the fact that Goethe, acknowledged to be one of the wisest of men, made Faust happy only when he was unselfishly interested in the welfare of others; and to remember that Benjamin Franklin, perhaps the shrewdest of all shrewd Americans, found the greatest pleasure of his long life in two things-public service and individual acts of kindness.

ANCIENT FOOTBALL

Attacks on the American game of football are often more sensational than the game itself. Some volley out statistics of injuries, in which we see the names of persons "crippled for life" whom we know to be unlike their biographers in that they are both well and cheerful; others descant wildly on the evils of betting and the drunkenness attendant upon a great match; others deplore the time and attention robbed from study; some believe the rivalry of two strong teams causes prolonged bitterness and hatred; some regard the intense earnestness of training as both silly and harmful; some assert that the players on the field behave like ruffians, and some, like the old Puritans, hate the game not because they really think it wicked but because they secretly hate to see eighty thousand people out for a holiday.

There is no doubt that football, like every other sport and recreation, is open to many serious objections. Certain players are every year killed and wounded, though the mortality is nothing like so great as that resulting from auto-mobile accidents and week-end celebrations. It is certainly true that betting and dissipation accompany the game; it is true that many young men sit on the benches, cheering and singing, when they might be studying in the seclusion of their rooms.

It is true that the American spirit-always ambitious of success-makes every member of a university team train with an earnestness that seems tragicomic to the nonathletic observer. But the immense advantages of this most robust of all sports outweigh all its attendant evils.

For football is much more than a contest of ani-mal vigour; in the language of Professor Stagg, who was a moralist before he was an athlete, "Football surpasses every other game in its demand for a high combination of physical, mental and moral qualities."

This article, however, is not written for the purpose of defending modern football but rather to show that the game thus far has not only flourished in spite of attacks but that there has been a tremendous rise in its respectability since the days of Queen Elizabeth. I cannot just now remember anything on which the Puritans and the playwrights were then agreed, except their opinion of football. What Shakespeare thought of it may be seen in the epithet which Kent applies to one of the most odious characters in *King Lear.* Tripping up Oswald, he calls him "you base football player."

Modern legislators must rejoice at finding that they have plenty of precedents for legal prohibition of the game. In 1424 we find "The King forbiddes that na man play fut ball under payne of iiiid." Sir Thomas Elyot remarked, in 1531,

"Foote balle, wherin is nothing but beastly furie and exstreme violence."

If in Elizabethan days the dramatists, who were not noted for their piety, attacked football, what shall we expect from the Puritans? The most circumstantial indictment of the game came from a Puritan of Puritans, Philip Stubbs.

In his *Anatomic of Abuses* (1583) he thus denounces the sport: For as concerning football playing, I protest unto you it may rather be called a frieendly kinde of fight, then a play of recreation; A bloody and murthering practise, then a felowly sporte or pastime. For dooth not euery one lye in waight for his Aduersarie, seek- ing to uerthrowe him & to picke him on his nose, though it be vppon hard stones? In ditch or dale, in valley or hil, or what place soeuer it be, hee careth not, so he haue him down. And he that can serue the most of this fashion, he is counted the only felow, and who but he? so that by this meanes, sometimes their necks are broken, sometimes their backs, some-time their legs, sometime their armes; sometime one part thrust out of ioynt, sometime another. Some-time the noses gush out with blood, sometime their eyes start out; and sometimes hurt in one place, some-times in another. But whosoever scapeth away the best, goeth not scotfree, but is either sore wounded, craised, and bruiseed so as he dyeth of it, or else scapeth very hardly, and no meruaile, for they haue the sleights to meet one betwixt two, to dash him against the hart with their elbowes, to hit him vnder the short ribbes with their griped fists, and with their knees to catch him vpon the hip, and to pick him on his neck, with a hundred such murdering devices; and hereof groweth enuie, malice, rancour, cholor, hatred, displeasure, enemities, and what not els; and some-times fighting, brawling, contention, quarrel picking, murther, homicide, and great effusion of blood, as experience dayely teacheth.

In the attack just quoted the most interesting thing to the modern reader is that precisely the same objections were made to the game as we hear today.

In the robust days of Queen Bess football was regarded as low and vulgar; it received the denunciation of the Church and the more potent frown of fashionable society. Today at a great university match prominent clergymen are seen even on the sidelines; the bleachers bloom with lovely women, and in a conspicuous place stands the President of the United States.

AN INSPIRING CEMETERY

Americans should not leave Florence without spending some reflective hours in the so-called Protestant cemetery. The grave of Elizabeth Barrett Browning is adorned with a beautiful marble tomb designed by the famous artist Leighton, and the only inscription thereupon is "E. B. B. Ob. 1861."

Not far away lies the famous poet, Walter Savage Landor, who died in 1864 at the age of eighty-nine. His grave is covered with a flat stone. Here is a poem he wrote about it:

> Twenty years hence, though it may hap
>
> That I be called to take a nap
>
> In a cool cell where thunder clap
>
> Was never heard,
>
> There breathe but o'er my arch of grass,
>
> A not too sadly sigh'd "Alas!"
>
> And I shall catch ere you can pass,

That winged word.

The last time I was in Florence I bent over his grave and with deliberate emphasis I whispered "Alas!" I do not know whether he heard me or not.

Robert and Elizabeth Browning made the poet's later years as happy as was possible for one of his temperament; they secured a villa for him, furnished it, hired servants and did what they could. He was wildly irascible, and if he did not like a meal that was served, he grabbed the tablecloth, and twitched all the food and dishes on to the floor. All his life he was a fighting man, which makes the beautiful Farewell he wrote somewhat incongruous.

THE LAST FRUIT OF AN OLD TREE

I strove with none; for none was worth my strife.

Nature I loved, and next to Nature, Art;

I warmed both hands before the fire of life.

It sinks and I am ready to depart.

In order to fit my own feelings, I should have to make some slight changes in his poem, so that the amended version would read as follows:

I strove with none. I always hated strife.

Nature I loved, and God and Man and Art.

I warmed both hands before the fire of life;

It sinks-yet I'm not ready to depart.

Landor was sometimes in a more jovial mood, as in his invitation to Tennyson

I entreat you, Alfred Tennyson,

Come and share my haunch of venison.

I have too a bin of claret,

Good, but better when you share it.

Tho' 'tis only a small bin,

There's a stock of it within.

And as sure as I'm a rhymer,

Half a butt of Rudesheimer.

Come; among the sons of men is one

Welcomer than Alfred Tennyson?

Along the path leading to Mrs. Browning's tomb is the grave of the English poet, Arthur Hugh Clough (pronounced Cluff), who crossed the ocean with Thackeray and James Russell Lowell and whose most famous poem is *Say Not the Struggle Nought Availeth.* He died in 1861 the same year as Mrs. Browning, at the early age of 42. He was a distinguished scholar of Balliol college, Oxford. He expressed in his poems the

doubts and struggles that have afflicted so many honest and candid minds.

Where lies the land to which the ship would go?

Far, far ahead, is all her seamen know.

And where the land she travels from? Away,

Far, far behind, is all that they can say.

On sunny noons upon the deck's smooth face,

Linked arm in arm, how pleasant here to pace;

Or, o'er the stern reclining, watch below

The foaming wake far widening as we go.

On stormy nights when wild northwesters rave,

How proud a thing to fight with wind and wave!

The dripping sailor on the reeling mast,

Exults to bear, and scorns to wish it past.

Where lies the land to which the ship would go?

Far, far ahead, is all her seamen know.

And where the land she travels from? Away.

Far, far behind, is all that they can say.

In addition to the three great English poets who are buried in this cemetery, two famous Americans lie there, Richard Hildreth and Theodore Parker. When I was an undergraduate, I asked Prof. W. G. Sumner what was the best History of the United States that had ever been written; he answered gruffly and without a word of qualification, "Hildreth's!" Accordingly, I read every word of the six volumes. Many years later I had the unique pleasure of telling Sumner something he had not known; I told him I had done homage at Hildreth's grave in Florence, and he was surprised to learn that the historian was buried there. If any one believes that the contemporary custom of "debunking" historical characters is new, he should read Hildreth's Preface to his History.

"Of centennial sermons and Fourth of July orations, whether professedly such or in the guise of history, there are more than enough. It is due to our fathers and ourselves, it is due to truth and phi-losophy, to present for once, on the historic stage, the founders of our American nation unbedaubed with patriotic rouge, wrapped up in no fine-spun cloaks of excuses and apology, without stilts, buskins, tinsel, or edizenment, in their own proper persons."

A PAIR OF SOCKS

One fine afternoon I was walking along Fifth Avenue, when I remembered that it was necessary to buy a pair of socks. Why I wished to buy only one pair is unimportant. I turned into the first sock shop that caught my eye, and a boy clerk who could not have been more than seventeen years old came forward. "What can I do for you, sir?" "I wish to buy a pair of socks." His eyes glowed. There was a note of passion in his voice. "Did you know that you had come into the finest place in the world to buy socks?" I had not been aware of that, as my entrance had been accidental. "Come with

me," said the boy, ecstatically. I followed him to the rear of the shop, and he began to haul down from the shelves box after box, displaying their contents for my delectation.

"Hold on, lad, I am going to buy only one pair!" "I know that," said he, "but I want you

to see how marvellously beautiful these are. Aren't they wonderful!" There was on his face an expression of solemn and holy rapture, as if he were revealing to me the mysteries of his religion.

I became far more interested in him than in the socks. I looked at him in amazement.

"My friend," said I, "if you can keep this up, if this is not merely the enthusiasm that

comes from novelty, from having a new job, if you can keep up this zeal and excitement day after day, in ten years you will own every sock in the United States."

My amazement at his pride and joy in salesmanship will be easily understood by all who read this article. In many shops the customer has to wait for some one to wait upon him. And when finally some clerk does deign to notice you, you are made to feel as if you were interrupting him. Either he is absorbed in profound thought in which he hates to be disturbed or he is sky-larking with a girl clerk and you feel like apologizing for thrusting yourself into such intimacy.

He displays no interest either in you or in the goods he is paid to sell. Yet possibly that very clerk who is now so apathetic began his career with hope and enthusiasm. The daily grind was too much for him; the novelty wore off; his only pleasures were found outside of working hours. He became a mechanical, not an inspired, salesman. After being mechanical, he became incompetent; then he saw younger clerks who had more zest in their work, promoted over him. He became sour and nourished a grievance.

That was the last stage. His usefulness was over. I have observed this melancholy decline in the lives of so many men in so many occupations that I have come to the conclusion that the surest road to failure is to do things mechanically.

There is, for example, no greater literature in the world than the Bible and no more exciting subject than religion. Yet I have heard many ministers of the gospel read the Bible in their churches with no interest and no emphasis, whereas they ought to read it as if they had just received it by wireless from Almighty God. I have heard hundreds of sermons preached mechanically, with no more appeal than if the speaker were a parrot. There are many teachers in schools and colleges who seem duller than the dullest of their pupils; they go through the motions of teaching, but they are as impersonal as a telephone.

In reading that remarkable book, *The Americanization of Edward Bok, I* was impressed by

what he said of competition m business. Beginning as a very young man in a certain occupation, he had expected to encounter the severest competition. As a matter of fact, he met no competition at all, and found that success was the easiest thing in the world, if one provided the conditions necessary for it.

He worked along with a number of other young men in the business. He was the only one who ever got to the place ahead of time. At the noon hour at lunch the other youngsters never on a single occasion mentioned the business in which they were engaged. They talked of their girls, or of athletic sports, or of various dissipations. He was the only man who ever remained after business hours, and he was convinced

that he was the only one who ever occupied his mind with the business during his evenings.

He rose above the others with consummate ease, and for two obvious reasons: First, he made himself indispensable; second, he found his chief pleasure in his work, not in the dissipations outside of it.

It is simple enough for any one to be attracted by the novelty of a new job. The real difficulty is to keep up that initial enthusiasm every day of one's life, to go to work every morning with zest and excitement. I believe that a man should live every day as if that day were his first and his last day on earth.

Every person needs some relaxation, some recreation; but a man's chief happiness should not lie outside his daily work, but in it. The chief difference between the happiness of child-hood and the happiness of maturity is that the child's happiness is dependent on something different from the daily routine-a picnic, an excursion, a break of some kind. But to the right sort of men and women happiness is found in

the routine itself, not in departures from it. Instead of hoping for a change, one hopes there will be no change, that one will have sufficient health to continue in one's chosen occupation.

The child has pleasures; the man has happiness. But unfortunately some men remain children all their lives.

APPRECIATION

As I DESCEND deeper into the vale of years, it becomes increasingly clear to me that I am a happier man not only than the average, but happier than many of those who are younger, healthier, stronger, and richer than I. And I say this after making due allowance for the fact that most people seem to hoard their happiness, as if they were afraid of spending it. They seem unwilling to look cheerful or to admit that they are happy.

Although the circumstances of my life have been fortunate, I believe the chief source of my happiness lies in my gift of appreciation. It is one more illustration of the law of causation. As I have ten times more appreciation than the average man or woman, it does not surprise me that I have more happiness.

On the ninth day of August 1712, Mr. Addison contributed a poem 'to the London Spectator which may be found today in nearly all the hymnbooks. It begins

"When all thy mercies, O my God, My rising soul surveys, Transported with the view, I'm lost in wonder, love, and praise."

Imagine a modern novelist or playwright or literary critic saying that! Imagine the average man or woman thinking it!

For, in the most tremendous age of miracles the world has ever known, the average man has lost his capacity for wonder. In a time when the world is drawn more closely together by common need than ever before, the majority of our writers have forgotten the meaning of the word love; while many regard the habit of praise as the mark of a shallow and plebeian mind.

Another stanza in Addison's poem is especially significant:

"Ten thousand thousand precious gifts My daily thanks employ,

Nor is the least a cheerful heart,"

That tastes those gifts with Joy. Addison thanked God for many precious gifts that came to him, but particularly because he had a cheerful heart. He could not have appreciated the panorama of life without that, any more than a blind man could appreciate the paintings of Rafael or a deaf man the songs of Schubert.

The prevention of disease consists in finding and removing the cause; the way to happiness consists in finding the key which will unlock the door of the prison in which so many of us dwell.

While a certain amount of money is essential merely to live, and the sum must be increased in order to

widen the range of one's enjoyment, it is unquestionably true that there are persons who apparently have everything and are not happy, while there are others with modest incomes and cheerful hearts.

As I can enjoy looking into a shop window without the slightest desire to possess anything it displays, so I believe one can enjoy many things without owning them or wishing to own them. If God offered to make me a present of the sunset, so that it would be my sunset, flare only on my property or flare more effectively on my property, I should decline to accept the gift. I appreciate the beauty of the sunset more than if I owned it.

I am not making the trite suggestion that instead of longing for what they have not got, people should make the best of what they have. There is hoary wisdom in such a suggestion, but it irritates more persons than it helps.

Appreciation as I understand it is something quite different and more rare. For by appreciation I mean to enjoy not only everything you possess but also everything else.

Appreciation is not self-satisfaction, complacency, or conceit. Those three qualities are centripetal, drawing all things toward the core of selfishness; while appreciation is centrifugal, throwing out ardours that make invisible contacts with beauty; forgetting oneself as completely as one does in listening to ravishing music.

The less satisfied one is with oneself (as distinguished from one's possessions) the more satisfied one will be with everything else; and the reverse is true.

The curse of modern life, the poison that turns honey to gall, the cause of the dull, stupid, despondent mood in which so many people live and move and have their being, is a lack of appreciation. Many go through life with their eyes, ears, and minds closed.

"Blessings brighten as they take their flight," said the Reverend Doctor Edward Young; but why should they? Why not consciously enjoy blessings while we have them, instead of spending our days and nights in vain regrets?

Life, with all its tragedy, frustration, disappointment, and unsatisfied desire is not so bad as many philosophers say it is. Very common experiences prove it. One may go to bed in a despondent frame of mind; but in the hour before dawn one has a horrible dream. One wakes up in a sweat of fear; then one hears the good old trolley-car go by, or the milkman leaving his bottles, and one rejoices; it is the cheerful, normal round. The dream was an hallucination. One is free. Real life seems good by contrast.

But real life seems good by contrast not only with horrors, but with a state of perfection. Ludwig Fulda wrote a play called Schlaraffenland where a wretched boy, clothed in rags, chronically cold and hungry in a miserable hovel, fell asleep and dreamed he was in a land of warm sunshine. Birds were flying very close to him and moving so slowly through the air that he reached out his hand and took one. It was a broiled chicken. He ate it with gusto, and another and another. Whenever he was hungry, the air was filled with perfectly cooked chickens. He looked at his rags-suddenly a broad door swung open, and there was a wardrobe filled with handsome and well-fitting clothes; all he had to do was to choose. Whatever desire he had was immediately gratified. For some time he was happy; then he began to be vaguely bored, dull, uninterested; this feeling of weariness gave way to increasing unhappiness. Finally, with a yell of agony he woke up-and found it was all a dream. He was cold, he was in rags, he was hungry; and as he looked around his miserable room, he exulted. "Thank God, I am back on the good old earth!"

Many men and women who find life melancholy and unsatisfying, suddenly catch the influenza. As the sufferer lies in bed with fever, unable to get up, he does not long for riches or fame or beauty or perfection. He wants only to be what he was last week. If he can have back his normal health and activity, it is all he asks. That state which a few days ago seemed nothing to be grateful for, now appears exceedingly good.

The point I make is, why wait for a bad dream, or an iridescent dream, or a fit of sickness to appreciate daily healthy existence? Why not enjoy these things while we have them? I mean consciously enjoy them. Well, I do.

G. K. Chesterton is profoundly religious; the late Arnold Bennett was not. But both men found rich enjoyment in daily living. They lived with gusto, with a keen relish. Arnold Bennett's attitude toward life was a chronic wonder, amazement, delight; even the innumerable little gadgets of modern existence pleased him enormously. While as for Mr. Chesterton, he says he hopes he will never be too old to stare at everything. Appreciation begets gratitude and gratitude begets happiness. You cannot store or save gratitude; economy there is fatal; if one tries to save gratitude, one may find it gone; but the more one gives, the more one has left. In the same number of the Spectator that contained his poem, Mr. Addison wrote, in the formal style of his day,

There is not a more pleasing exercise of the mind than gratitude. It is accompanied with such an inward

satisfaction, that the duty is sufficiently rewarded by the performance. It is not like the practice of many other virtues, difficult and painful, but attended with so much pleasure, that . . . a generous mind would indulge in it, for the natural gratification that accompanies it.

Even as a little child, I responded gratefully-and usually with surprise -to any acts of kindness or to any courtesies from older people. Even now I find no difficulty in feeling appreciation for generosity, hospitality, or praise; my grateful response is as spontaneous as the deed or word which it acknowledges. On a certain occasion many years ago another college professor and I were entertained at a magnificent house over the weekend. When we came to go, it was as natural as breathing for me to express to our hostess how much I appreciated her kindness; and I meant it. I told her I should never forget it, and I never have forgotten it. My colleague, being of a quite different temperament, looked at the lady and spoke one word-" Good-bye."

When we had left the place, he said "What a horrible effort it is to be polite! and it doesn't bother you at all." Now this man is a staunch and loyal friend-only he does not get half the fun out of life that I do, because he has no gift of appreciation.

I must have been born with an unlimited gift of appreciation; and it has grown by what it feeds on. It may be that I am too easily pleased -that I have not a sufficient amount of discrimination. I admire summer and winter, sunrises and sunsets, I like moonlight and even better star light, I enjoy classic and Gothic and Colonial architecture, I like great tragedies, great comedies, great farces, I revere the courage of a Ney and the courage of a washerwoman. If I were more fastidious, if only a very few objects and only a very few persons received my approval, then perhaps I should have a higher reputation as a discerning critic. And if I almost never praised anything, then on the rare occasions when I did, even though somewhat grudgingly, release admiration, my praise would be worth more than it is now. But think of all the happiness I should lose! Many ignorant men believe criticism means fault-finding. They think the best critic of a poem or a play or a composition of music, is the man who searches sedulously for defects and limitations, rather than the man who discerns what is good and praises it. I am willing to admit that some books and plays please me that evoke no admiration in others.

And many books and plays, which are highly praised by others, disgust me beyond words; which is why I can find no words to express my opinion of them. I believe the best praise one can give any work of the imagination is to say it is worth criticising; and by criticism I mean neither faultfinding nor denunciation. The art of criticism is the art of interpretation; interpretation requires insight.

Furthermore, while I get more happiness out of the gift of appreciation than I should from being overfastidious, I must admit there are certain persons who seem to find sincere pleasure in depreciating and ridiculing every book they read, every play they see, every musical performance they hear. Various attempts at creative art are valuable to these critics as a target is valuable to a marksman, or a head at Donnybrook Fair. It is an opportunity for the exercise of destructive wit; I suppose there is a certain pleasure in wielding a bludgeon -the joy of the slapstick. Some critics obtain pleasure not only in this exercise, "Gregory, remember thy swashing blow," but in the reputation in this fashion acquired; yes, even in the fear they inspire. For while most people are neither formidable nor dangerous, most people secretly like to be so regarded. It may be a damaging admission; but no man, woman, or child has ever been afraid of me.

Yet, granting the definite pleasure in conscienceless murder, I do not believe that the critic whose main weapons are irony, sarcasm, and ridicule, gets half the fun out of life that I have. And I also believe that this attitude of depreciation, except where it is accompanied with constructive suggestions, is usually sterile. These are the critics whom Thomas Hardy called "sworn discouragers of effort."

Indiscriminate praise-even indiscriminate sympathy-would, in matters of art, be worthless. But the fact that I prefer to spend my time and energy in the appreciation of good things rather than in the denunciation of unworthiness, does not mean that I am without a standard. It does not take me long to discover that in a package of ten new novels, nine ought not to have been published; that (judging by the advertisements) of motion pictures, the majority are vulgar; that when I turn on the radio to hear something I am eager to hear, I wheel my way to it through a morass so sickening that it seems as if it must produce softening of the brain.

Indeed, I think some of our modern writers have no standards at all. Their pictures of slime are of little value because there is no suggestion that there ought to be, as of course there is, a higher level of character and environment. Dickens gave us pictures of low life, but we always knew by reading his pages that it was "low" because it could be measured by an experience of what was better. Mr. Santayana commends Dickens because he always knew the difference between right and wrong. His good people are really good, his evil people are really bad. I do not believe a novelist, playwright, or critic can judge human nature if he does not know any difference between right and wrong.

The greatest of all German critics, Goethe, said the chief qualification for a critic was Enthusiasm. I believe this to be true. A critic of music must begin by loving music; a drama critic must begin by loving the theatre; a literary critic must begin by loving books. Love is the foundation of understanding; and enthusiasm the wellspring of intelligent appreciation. Is it not possible that some critics who began by loving their chosen field of art have gradually lost that love; and with the loss of enthusiasm has vanished also quickness of insight, sensitiveness to impressions?

And if this is true in matters of art -music, theatre, books-it is surely true of life itself. One reason so many people are not so happy as they ought to be is not because of their lack of material things-but because they do not respond to beauty in nature, and charm in men and women, as they used to. The power of appreciation should grow with one's advance through life; life itself does not grow less mysterious, less beautiful, less interesting; it is not the object, but sight and hearing that are dull. If you find you are not so much interested "in things" as you used to be, the trouble is with you, and must be corrected. Fortunately it can be.

Encouragement is creative; irony is destructive. Encouragement does not mean falsehood, and I am not suggesting that one should say a manuscript, a book, a picture, a singing voice is good when one inwardly knows it to be otherwise.

But as a professional teacher, I have had abundant opportunity to observe the developing power of encouragement and the sterilizing effect of scorn. People endeavour to live up to praise and to justify it; whereas cynicism or indifference will often extinguish a faint spark of talent. I remember, more than thirty years ago, asking a student to remain a moment after class; I told him his written work was excellent, far superior to the average. His face was flooded with surprise and joy. He said in all his years in school and college that was the first time any teacher had given him a word of encouragement. Well, his subsequent career more than proved his worth. But the point I make is, that while my passing comment gave him happiness, his happiness in receiving it was not so great as mine in giving it. And the main object of this little book is to show that one road to happiness lies through appreciation.

Most men and women do not sufficiently realise the sensitiveness of our fellow-creatures. J. M. Barrie says that sometimes, after having read a venomous attack on his work, he has written a bitter rejoinder (which he knows how to do), gone out into the street to post it, and with his hand over the letter-box, suddenly reflected that perhaps his victim will receive this epistle after he has sat up all night with a sick child, or after he has just received a shattering financial disaster or after the physician has told him he has a fatal disease.

Now, while most men and women are not in an acute crisis of tragedy, everyone has something to worry about. I do not care to add to his torment. The reason I do not exercise the power of adverse criticism is not because of lack of ability. Mr. Addison said the reason he did not tell vile stories was not because he did not know any. My ability to hurt another man's feelings is quite sufficient. Once I was urged by the editor of a college paper to criticise the contributed articles severely-" Please be unmerciful; it will do them good!"

Accordingly I selected one short story for especial condemnation. The undergraduate author himself gave no hint that he was hurt. It was one of his friends who told me that it was the first time this man had ever had anything in print; he had feared it was not good; and my censure had hurt him so that he would never try again. It appeared that he had a natural tendency to discouragement and low spirits; a few years later he committed suicide. It is not pleasant for me to reflect that during his short life I had added to his suffering.

It is surprising to those who have not fully considered the weaknesses of human nature how very sensitive are the majority of human beings. Many people, both great and small, prominent and obscure, seem unable to endure adverse comment, irony, ridicule, insult, without intense and prolonged suffering. To say of any person that he was harmless would seem such faint praise as almost to make him ridiculous; he might feel justified in resenting it. But really, if such an adjective could accurately be applied to any man or woman-it never can-it would be a marvellous tribute.

We hurt somebody almost every day; intent upon our own purposes, we jostle and shove our way through the complexities of social intercourse, leaving wounds more acute than if we jammed an elbow into somebody's eye.

No decent man would kick a cripple; but there are many who suffer more from ridicule and adverse criticism, yes, even from lack of consideration, than they would from a bodily injury. There are many unfortunate men and women who have no particularly sensitive spot, because every spot is sensitive.

Even men of genius have confessed that they suffer more from one adverse criticism than they gain in happiness by ten favorable reviews. I was amazed when I learned that writers of established fame-Tennyson, Hardy, Henry James-suffered excruciatingly from attacks by reviewers whose opinion was of no importance. If gold rust, what shall iron do?

If men and women of talent and popularity are so sensitive to an ill wind, what must be the anguish of those who are not sure of themselves, who are struggling hard, and with constant misgiving, to do better work? I know as a matter of fact that there are many distinguished artists who never read a word written about them, because they cannot endure an unfavourable remark.

Hence when a young actor or singer or playwright or composer takes up a newspaper and sees himself held up as an object of derision, he suffers torture inexpressible. A woman whose first play was savagely reviewed wrote me that when one fails in business or in athletic attempts, people are sympathetic; but when one writes a play that fails, the critics put the playwright in a position as if he had done something shameful in the presence of the public.

Anyone who writes a book or a play certainly invites attack; it is as if he stood stripped and bound in the marketplace, where every passer had a right to throw something at him. "Oh, that mine adversary had written a book!"

Once more, I do not mean that a critic, in order to spare the feelings of anyone, should dishonestly praise what is not worth praising. But in transfixing a victim with the critical pen, it is not necessary to put poison on the tip. And wherever it is possible to give encouragement or to see a high purpose even through failure, it is well to remember the good results that come from sympathetic insight and appreciation.

This need not be applied only to professional criticism. It applies to the give and take of daily life. Every boy and girl, every man and woman is an object of observation and therefore of criticism. Appreciation stimulates and depreciation discourages. Most men and women need courage.

In these matters as in the general question of happiness, I am more fortunate than the majority of people; because in the first place I am more pleased by praise than I am downcast by blame; and in the second place, abuse and slander and misrepresentation do not give me deep or lasting pain. When it has been my unpleasant occupation to read or hear harsh attacks on something I have said or written or done-attacks meant to be devastating, to destroy my peace of mind-these blows annoy me no more than mosquito bites. If I refrain from scratching, the poison will not sink in, the bite will soon be forgotten. As soon as an injury is forgotten, it is as if it never had been. Adverse attacks and ridicule are not agreeable, but one can train oneself to endure them; even to feel no prolonged resentment.

Here again is the enormous blessing that comes from hard work. I am really too busy to spend much time contemplating my bruises. There is always the next thing that must be done.

The late Commodore William J. Matheson, one of the most interesting men I ever knew, read to me an abusive letter he had just received. I made the conventional remark "Don't let it worry you!" He looked at me in astonishment: "Why, such things never worry me. You can see by the letter that it is the other fellow who is doing all the worrying!" We exaggerate the power of our enemies and the importance of their attacks. Many persons who have been "criticised" imagine that everybody on the street is thinking of their predicament; but no, these people are all thinking of something else.

One should make the most of all sources of happiness no matter how trivial they may seem; they are not trivial if they produce joy. When I was a schoolboy, I enjoyed the Saturday holiday so much-every Saturday-that along about three o'clock on every Friday afternoon I felt a rising tide of bliss-the bliss of anticipation. And as I have never been easily disappointed, Saturday was usually just as good as I thought it would be. Outdoor games and all that sort of thing-winter and summerwere an inexpressible delight. As for tremendous events, like Christmas and the Fourth of July, they were a delirium.

Yet as I look back on childhood and youth, happy though I was, I have no regret that they are irrevocable; I have no sentimental yearning for the past. I walked and ran and skipped and leaped through those flowery roads and advanced into a country quite different but more interesting; because there was not only more to appreciate, but my power of appreciation had developed.

The difference between my happiness as a child and my happiness as a man, is that then I always wanted something unusual to happen, some excitement to take me out of the routine. Saturday was the golden day of the week. Now my hope is that nothing different will happen. I hope only I may be able to keep in sufficient health or vigour to go on with the daily routine. Instead of waiting for the holiday, every day is interesting. I enjoy the hot bath in the tub as I used to enjoy the old swimming hole.

Perhaps those men and women who are still looking for excitement, something with a "kick" in it, are mature only in body. They have not developed.

Perhaps in their search for excitement, they are neglecting sources of happiness more easily attainable. For as many persons are either afraid or unwilling to admit that they are happy, so many men and women are ashamed or afraid to admit their appreciation of simple and ordinary things. True mental development consists largely in the discovery of what has been there all the time. It may be as I have said-that I am not sufficiently discriminating; yet experience proves to me that my enjoyment of elementary means of entertainment does not detract from my enjoyment of the best; even though I enjoy the best more than the second best.

I am transported by the symphonies of Beethoven and by the operas of Wagner. Yet that does not lessen my enjoyment of Gilbert and Sullivan, of a drum and fife corps, of a brass band. As I grow older, I find Shakespeare constantly more thrilling; the beauty and felicity of his language are enchanting; yet I have tremendous relish out of a good detective story. I shall never forget my excitement in seeing Edwin Booth in The Merchant of Venice, yet I love the circus and everything in it.

I admire Lindbergh and all spectacular heroes; and I admire humble men and women, who, in adverse circumstances, show courage and cheerfulness in obscurity. Browning said, "

O world as God has made it! all is beauty: And knowing this is love, and love is duty."

Nature is always beautiful; and as one becomes older, nature becomes more and more beautiful. I am writing these words in New York. From my room on the sixteenth story I saw the sun rise over the East River this morning, and my heart exulted.

THE END

A PRIVATE LIBRARY ALL YOUR OWN

A borrowed book is like a guest in the house; it must be treated with punctiliousness, with a certain considerate formality. You must see that it sustains no damage; it must not suffer while under your roof. You cannot leave it carelessly, you cannot mark it, you cannot turn down the pages, you cannot use it familiarly. And then, some day, although this is seldom done, you really ought to return it.

But your own books belong to you; you treat them with that affectionate intimacy that annihilates formality. Books are for use, not for show; you should own no book that you are afraid to mark up, or afraid to place on the table, wide open and face down. A good reason for marking favourite passages in books is that this practice enables you to remember more easily the significant sayings, to refer to them quickly, and then in later years, it is like visiting a forest where you once blazed a trail. You have the pleasure of going over the old ground, and recalling both the intellectual scenery and your own earlier self.

Everyone should begin collecting a private library in youth; the instinct of private property, which is fundamental in human beings, can here be cultivated with every advantage and no evils. One should have one's own bookshelves, which should not have doors, glass windows, or keys; they should be free and accessible to the hand as well as to the eye. The best of mural decorations is books; they are more varied in colour and appearance than any wall-paper, they are more attractive in design, and they have the prime advantage of being separate personalities, so that if you sit alone in the room in the firelight, you are surrounded with intimate friends. The knowledge that they are there in plain view is both stimulating and refreshing. You do not have to read them all. Most of my indoor life is spent in a room containing six thousand books; and I have a stock answer to the invariable question that comes from strangers. "Have you read all of these books?" "Some of them twice." This reply is both true and unexpected.

There are of course no friends like living, breathing, corporeal men and women; my devotion to reading has never made me a recluse. How could it? Books are of the people, by the people, for the people. Literature is the immortal part of history; it is the best and most enduring part of personality. But book-friends have this advantage over living friends; you can enjoy the most truly aristocratic society in the world whenever you want it. The great dead are beyond our physical reach, and the great living are usually almost as inaccessible; as for our personal friends and acquaintances, you cannot always see them. Perchance they are asleep, or away on a journey.

But in a private library, you can at any moment converse with Socrates or Shakespeare or Carlyle or Dumas or Dickens or Shaw or Barrie or Galsworthy. And there is no doubt that in these books you see these men at their best. They wrote for YOU. They "laid themselves out," they did their ultimate best to entertain you, to make a favourable impression. You are necessary to them as an audience is to an actor; only instead of seeing them masked, you look into their inmost heart of heart. The "'real Charles Dickens" is in his novels, not in his dressing-room.

Everyone should have a few reference books, carefully selected, and within reach. I have a few that I can lay my hands on without leaving my chair; this is not because I am lazy, but because I am busy.

One should own an Authorised Version of the Bible in big type, a good one-volume dictionary, the one-volume *Index and Epitome* to the *Dictionary of National Biography,* a one-volume History of England and another of the United States, Ryland's *Chronological Outlines of English Literature,* Whitcomb's *Chronological Outlines of American Literature,* and other works of reference according to one's special tastes and pursuits. These reference books should be, so far as possible, up to date.

The works of poets, dramatists, novelists, essayists, historians, should be selected with care, and should grow in number in one's private library from the dawn of youth to the day of death.

First editions are an expensive luxury, but are more interesting to the average mind than luxurious bindings. When you hold in your hand a first edition of the seventeenth century, you are reading that book in its proper time-setting; you are reading it as the author's contemporaries read it; maybe your copy was handled by the author himself. Furthermore, unless you have paid too much for it, it is usually a good investment; it increases in value more rapidly than stocks and shares, and you have the advantage of using it. It is great fun to search book catalogues with an eye to bargains; it is exciting to attend an auction sale.

But of course most of us must be content to buy standard authors, living and dead, in modern editions. Three qualities are well to bear in mind. In getting any book, get the complete edition of that book; not a clipped, or condensed, or improved or paraphrased version. Second, always get books in black, clear, readable type. When you are young, you don't mind; youth has the eyes of eagles. But later, you refuse to submit to the effort-often amounting to pain involved in reading small type, and lines set too close together. Third, get volumes that are light in weight. It is almost always possible to secure this inestimable blessing in standard authors. Some books are so heavy that to read them is primarily a gymnastic, rather than mental exercise; and if you travel, and wish to carry them in your bag or trunk, they are an intolerable burden.

Refuse to submit to this. There was a time when I could tell, merely by "hefting" it, whether a book had been printed in England or in America; but American publishers have grown in grace, and today many American books are easy to hold.

Some books must be bought in double column; but avoid this wherever possible, and buy such books only when economy makes it necessary to have the complete works of the author in one volume. A one-volume Shakespeare is almost a necessity; but it should be used for reference, as we use a dictionary, never for reading. Get Shakespeare in separate volumes, one play at a time.

It is better to have some of an author's works in attractive form, than to have them complete in a cumbrous or ugly shape.

Remember that for the price of one ticket to an ephemeral entertainment, you can secure a book that will give strength and pleasure to your mind all your life. Thus I close by saying two words to boys and girls, men and women: BUY BOOKS.

A ROOM WITHOUT A VIEW

What is the worst poem ever written by a man of genius? It is certain that if an anthology should be made of the most terrible verses of the English bards the results would be both surprising and appalling. I cannot at this moment think of any worse pair of lines in English literature than those offered in all seriousness by the seventeenth-century poet, Richard Crashaw. They occur in a poem containing many lovely passages. In comparing the tearful eyes of Mary Magdalene to many different things he perpetrated a couplet more remarkable for ingenuity than for beauty. Her eyes are

Two walking baths, two weeping motions,
Portable and compendious oceans.

Alfred Tennyson, in his second volume of poems, bearing the date 1833, included the following, though it is only fair to say that he afterward suppressed it. It aroused the mirth of the critics and still is often resurrected as a specimen of what Tennyson could do when he was deserted by both inspiration and taste.

O DARLING ROOM

0 darling room, my heart's delight,

Dear room, the apple of my sight,
With thy two couches soft and white,
There is no room so exquisite,

No little room so warm and bright,
Wherein to read, wherein to write.

For I the Nonnenwerth have seen,
And Oberwinter's vineyards green,
Musical Lurlei; and between
The hills to Bingen have I been,
Bingen in Darmstadt,
where the Rhene Curves toward Mentz, a woody scene.

Yet never did there meet my sight,
In any town, to left or right,
A little room so exquisite,
With two such couches soft and white;
Not any room so warm and bright,
Wherein to read, wherein to write.

Imagine the profanity and laughter this piffle must have aroused among the book reviewers; some of his severer critics called him "Miss Alfred," not knowing that he was a six-footer, with a voice like a sea captain in a fog.

I have no mind to defend the poem. Apart from the fact that the reading of it ought to teach Americans the correct accent on the word "exquisite," it must be admitted that when Tennyson wrote this stuff he not only nodded but snored.

But, although it is difficult for me to understand how he could have written it, have read it in proof and then published it, I perfectly understand and sympathise with his enthusiasm for the room.

It is often said that polygamous gentlemen are-at any rate, for a considerable periodmonogamous; the Turk may have a long list of wives, but he will cleave to one, either because he wants to or because she compels him to. Thus, even in a house that has a variety of sitting rooms, or living rooms or whatever you choose to call them, the family will use only one. After the evening meal they will instinctively move toward this one favourite room.

There is no doubt that even as dogs and cats have their favourite corner or chair, or favourite cushion of nightly repose, men and women have favourite rooms. And if this is true of a family in general, it is especially true of a man or a woman whose professional occupation is writing; and he becomes so attached to his room that Tennyson's sentiments, no matter how silly in expression, accurately represent his emotion.

Twice a year, once in June and once in September, circumstances force me to leave a room

where I have for a long time spent the larger part of my waking hours; I always feel the pain of parting, look around the walls and at the desk and wish the place an affectionate farewell, hoping to see it again, either in the autumn or in the next summer, as the case may be. I love that room, as Tennyson loved his room. I love it not because of the view from the windows, for a working room should not have too good a view, but for the visions that have there appeared to the eyes of the mind. It is the place where I have sat in thought, where such ideas as are possible to my limited range have appeared to me and where I have endeavoured to express them in words.

And if I can have so strong a passion for a room, with what tremendous intensity must an inspired poet or novelist love the secluded chamber where his imagination has found free play!

We know that Hawthorne, after his graduation from college, spent twelve years in one room in Salem. When he revisited that room as a famous writer he looked at it with unspeakable affection and declared that if ever he had a biographer great mention must be made in his memoir of this chamber, for here his mind and character had been formed and here the immortal children of his fancy had played around him. He was alone and not alone. As far as a mortal man may understand the feelings of a man of genius, I understand the emotion of Hawthorne.

I think nearly every one, if he were able to afford it, would like to have a room all his own. I believe it to be an important factor in the development of the average boy or girl if in the family house each child could have one room sacred to its own personality. When I was a small boy, although I loved to be with family and friends, I also loved to escape to my own room and read and meditate in solitude.

The age of machinery is not so adverse to spiritual development as the age of hotels and apartment houses; there is no opportunity for solitude, and a certain amount of solitude, serene and secure from interruption, is almost essential for the growth of the mind. A great many girls and women could be saved from the curse of "nerves" if there were a place somewhere in the building where they could be for a time alone. One of the worst evils of poverty is that there is no solitude; eating, sleeping, living, all without privacy.

When I was a graduate student in the university I was fortunate enough to possess for one year exactly the right kind of room. The young philosopher, George Santayana, came to see me and exclaimed, "What a perfect room for a scholar! The windows high up, as they should be." For if one is to have clear mental vision it is not well that the room should have a view.

ATHLETICS

The whole world, with the exception of India, China, Siberia and a few other countries, has gone wild over athletics. Although new stadiums and amphitheatres are in process of construction everywhere, it is impossible to accommodate the crowds. Millions of people have apparently the money and the time to devote to these spectacular contests, and many more millions "listen in" on the radio. In England last June Wimbledon was not half large enough to hold the frantic crowd that wished to see the tennis matches; the same is true of France. At a recent wrestling contest in Austria, after all the seats were taken, the gates were broken down by the mob of spectators who wished to enter; about 150,000 people saw a prize fight in Chicago and it is significant of the times that the only vacant seats were the cheapest.

Every newspaper devotes an immense amount of space to sporting news; and all the leading daily journals employ a highly paid staff of experts on sports, who keep the public agog with excitement before every contest and who endeavour to satisfy its curiosity after the battle is over.

Now there are some pessimistic philosophers who look upon all this athletic fever as a sign of degeneration, as evidence of the coming eclipse of civilisation. They point out that during the decay of the Roman Empire there was a universal excitement over sports, and they draw the inference that European and American civilisation is headed toward disaster.

No one can read the future, although innumerable fakers are paid for doing so. But it is at least possible that the ever-growing interest in athletics, instead of being a sign of degeneration, is in reality one more proof of the gradual domination of the world by Anglo-Saxon language, customs and ideas.

Extreme interest in athletics, though it can-not be defended on strictly rational grounds, is not necessarily accompanied by a lack or loss of interest in intellectual matters. If one had to name the place and the time when civilisation reached its climax, one might well name Athens in the fifth century before Christ. If one compares Athenian public interest in the tragedies of Sophocles with New York public interest in musical comedy, the contrast is not flattering to American pride. Yet that intellectual fervour in Athens was accompanied by a tremendous interest in track athletics. Every Greek city was a separate state; their only bond of union was the track meet held every four years and called the Olympic Games, to which the flower of youth from every Greek town contributed; and the winner of each event-a simon-pure amateur, receiving as prize only a laurel wreath was a hero for at least four years.

From the strictly rational point of view it is impossible to defend or even to explain the universal ardour over athletics, but it is best to regard it as a fact, and then see what its causes are.

The majority of Anglo-Saxons have always had sporting blood, and the Latin races are now being infused with it. I well remember a train journey near Chicago during the darkest days of the World War. We were all awaiting the newspapers. Suddenly a newsboy entered and we bought eagerly. The man sitting next to me was a clergyman in Episcopal uniform. He looked not at the front part of the paper, but. turned feverishly to the sporting page, which he read carefully. When I called on the Very Reverend Dean of Rochester Cathedral, in England, Dean Hole, I was shown into a room con taining several thousand books. I glanced over these and all I saw dealt exclusively with sport. Many excellent men without sporting blood have protested against the domination of athletics. The famous English novelist, Wilkie Collins, published a novel, *Man and Wife,* which was a protest against the British love of sports, in which both athletes and the public were ridiculed. Why should thousands pay money to see two men run a race? What difference did it make to civilisation which man won?

Yet, although it is easy to overdo excitement about athletics, the growing interest in sport which has been so characteristic of France, Germany and Italy during the last ten years is a good thing for the youth of these countries and for their national and international temper.

Years ago, the space occupied in England and in America by fields devoted to various outdoor sports was in Germany and France used for public gardens, where people sat and drank liquor while listening to a band or watching some vaudeville. When I first travelled on the Continent, I found only one tennis court and that was at Baden-Baden. Today one finds everywhere in France and Germany tennis courts, golf links and football fields.

It is surely not a change for the worse that a German student who used to test his physical endurance by the number of quarts of beer he could drink at a sitting tests it today in tennis, rowing and football, and that the French students with silky beards, who used to strain their eyes looking at women, now, clean-shaven and alert, are looking at the tennis ball.

It is, of course, irrational to take an eager interest in a prize fight, but if you have sporting blood you cannot help it. My father was an orthodox Baptist minister. As I had never heard him mention prize fighting, I supposed he took no interest in it.

But the day after a famous battle, as I was reading aloud the newspaper to him, I simply read the headline, "Corbett

Defeats Sullivan," and was about to pass on to something important when my father leaned forward and said earnestly, "Read it by rounds."

A VISIBLE CHURCH IN AN INVISIBLE TOWN

Looking at a map of Lower Michigan, one will see it is shaped like a mitten on the left hand, with a distinctly marked Thumb. The Thumb-Nail is Huron County, the county town being Bad Axe, and the old railroad terminus being Grindstone; the nearness of the two places inspiring obvious pleasantries. Four miles east of Grindstone is Huron City, once a fairly large and prosperous lumbering village, and now so small that strangers drive through it without seeing it. Many have motored on ten miles in the vain endeavour to find it.

Mr. Langdon Hubbard, of Bloomfield, Conn., founded the town in the 'fifties, made roads through the forests, and built the first pier. Eighty years ago he made it possible to have regular services. For a long time the schoolhouse served this purpose, but in 1885 Mr. Hubbard made provision for a church edifice, which has been open since that date. The Methodist minister assigned to this 'charge' preaches in three places; in the morning at Redman, eight miles away, in the afternoon at Huron City, and in the evening at Port Hope, where he lives. In the days of horses, this was a serious undertaking; for the roas were never good, even in the best of summer weather, and for the rest of the year they were almost incredibly bad. But with the advent of the Ford Car, all this has been changed. Now we have excellent roads, and the Huron City Church is easily accessible to those who live within a radius of a hundred miles or more.

I wish the following account of a successful experiment might induce summer visitors from city to country elsewhere not to be content with merely taking rest and recreation, but to give as well as receive – to identify themselves with the life of rural communities, and if they have any talent for usefulness, to employ that in summer service. Browning says,

God uses us to help each other so, Lending our minds out.

Many religious people dream of a genuine Christian Community Church, where devout people from various denominations and sects will worship together without any self-consciousness; that is, without being aware that they are doing anything unusual. What ought to be common is extremely rare.

Yet in our Huron City Church, to use Kipling's phrase, 'the thing that couldn't has occurred.' Representatives from all the churches, together with many others, come cheerfully to Huron City every Sunday afternoon in July, August, and September.

The automobile had made it unnecessary to seek a good or convenient location for a church; any location will do; if the services are interesting and beneficial, people will come.

Attending Church in Huron City in the 1920s

I have been asked, 'Why do you preach to such a collection of sects? Do you give a literary lecture or a moral talk?' My answer is that I preach only the simple gospel and nothing else; and there being so many members of so many sects in the audience, I leave out non-essentials and dogmas peculiar to individual churches (winds of doctrine) and stick close to the central theme of the New Testament.

No member of the congregation enjoys this church more than I. As I go into the pulpit and look over that audience of hard-working farmers, their wives and babies, and know that they and many others have given up their Sunday afternoon and motored many miles to be present, I feel a thrill unspeakable.

There is no formality about this church and there is no one to greet visitors with a professional smile and handclasp; people enter this building as they enter their own home, knowing there will be neither coldness nor officious effusiveness. Nor are they ever urged to come again; they will come again when they feel like it.

On one occasion immediately after the service, when nearly everyone had gone outside, an over-enthusiastic gentleman came up to the pulpit and said emphatically, 'I want you to know that I'm a Unitarian! I don't care one whoop for the damn dogmas you people believe; but I like this church; it's the first time I've been here; and I want to give fifty dollars to it; so long as you understand that I am a Unitarian!' Although his excitement had an alcoholic foundation, he showed his interest in a practical way; for the collections taken during the summer support this church during the barren winter months. He wrote his cheque in a firm hand; I thanked him, and saw him no more. Before adding it to our contributions, however, I made enquiries to see if he could afford it, as I did not wish him to regret his good impulse after his zeal had cooled. I found that he was abundantly able to spare the fifty dollars.

Then I sat down and wrote a letter to the most ardent Unitarian in America, Chief Justice William Howard Taft. 'There was a Unitarian in our Methodist Church last Sunday; he seemed abnormally excited, but he was a thorough gentleman, for he contributed fifty dollars.' I immediately received a reply: 'I am not surprised there was a Unitarian in your Methodist Church; and I am not very much surprised that he was excited; but I am amazed that you got fifty dollars out of him. I never knew any Unitarian who was that much ahead.'

William Lyon Phelps - 1939

BIRDS AND STATESMEN

When, in the Spring of 1910, Theodore Roosevelt was on his way to England from his African explorations, he wrote a strange letter to the British Foreign Office in London. I call it a strange letter, because it is the kind of epistle one would not expect to be sent by an ex-executive of one country to the Foreign Office of another. He wrote that during his stay in England he would like to make an excursion into the woods, hear the English songbirds and learn their names; in order that he might do this satisfactorily and intelligently, would the Foreign Office please select some naturalist who knew the note of every bird in England and request him to accompany Mr. Roosevelt on this expedition?

Well, the head of the British Foreign Office was Sir Edward Grey and he himself knew the note of every singing bird in England-a remarkable accomplishment for one of the busiest statesmen in the world. He therefore appointed himself as bird-guide for the ex-President of the United States.

The two distinguished men stood on a railway platform one day in May and were surrounded by reporters, who supposed that a new world problem of the first magnitude was on the carpet. But the two men told the reporters that they were going away into the country for two days, did not wish to be disturbed, and asked the journalists to leave them alone. Accordingly, it was generally believed that Roosevelt and Grey were absorbed in the discussion of international affairs, and as the great war broke out a few years later, some went so far as to believe then that it had its origin in this sinister interview.

Now, as a matter of fact, the two men did not mention either war or politics; they went awalking in the New Forest and every time they heard the voice of a bird, Grey told Roosevelt the singer's name. They both agreed (and so do I) that the English blackbird is the best soloist in Great Britain.

It is a curious fact that the four most famous birds in English literature are none of them native in America. The Big Four are the Nightingale, the Skylark, the Blackbird and the Cuckoo. From Chaucer to Kipling the British poets have chanted the praise of the Nightingale. And of all the verses in his honour, it is perhaps the tribute by Keats that is most worthy of the theme.

> Thou was not born for death, immortal Bird!
> No hungry generations tread thee down;
> The voice I hear this passing night was heard
> In ancient days by emperor and clown:
> Perhaps the self-same song that found a path

Through the sad heart of Ruth, when, sick for home,

She stood in tears amid the alien corn;

The same that oftimes hath
Charmed magic casements,
opening on the foam Of perilous seas,
in faery lands forlorn.

We never had nightingales in the United States until Edward W. Bok imported them into his Bird Paradise in Florida. Previous attempts to bring them over had failed; the birds invariably died. Some investigators declared that this tragedy was owing to the change of diet; but of course the real reason for their death was American poetry. After the nightingales had listened for centuries to Chaucer, Shakespeare, Milton, Wordsworth, Keats, etc., the change to the level of American verse was too much for them, and they died of shock.

The English skylark leaves the grass and soars aloft, singing his heart out, so that after he has disappeared in the sky, we hear his voice coming down out of the blue, like a revelation. One of the poets calls it a "sightless song." Shakespeare sends the skylark to the gate of heaven.

And Shelley's poem on the skylark expresses the ethereal nature of the soaring voice of this bird

Higher still and higher

From the earth thou springest,

Like a cloud o[fire;

The blue deep thou wingest,

And singing still dost soar,

and Soaring ever singest.

little face, he sent straight into the gale the loveliest music. Tennyson has observed how the voice of the blackbird loses its beauty in the hot Summer days.

A golden bill! the silver tongue,
Cold February loved, is dry:
Plenty corrupts the melody
That made thee famous once, when young;
And in the sultry garden-squares,
Now thy flute-notes are changed to coarse,
I hear thee not at all, or hoarse
As when a hawker hawks his wares.

American blackbirds do not sing well; the socalled crow-blackbird, so common in flocks in autumn, makes a noise like tonsillitis, or as if he had a boy's voice in process of changing, or as if he were a hinge that needed oiling. Our redwing blackbird, with his scarlet epaulets, has a good-natured and perky wheeze, which can hardly be called singing. But the English and Continental blackbird pours out of his throat the most heavenly melody. One Winter day in Munich, in the midst of a snowstorm, I saw a blackbird perched on a tree directly in front of the University building. He was "hove to," that is, he had his beak turned directly into the wind, and as the snowflakes beat against his

The nearest we Americans can get to the English cuckoo is the abominable cuckoo clock. The voice of the English cuckoo sounds exactly like the clock, only of course you can't train him to strike right. In addition to his regular accomplishment, he is a ventriloquist and can throw his voice a tremendous distance. One day, crossing a field in Sussex, I heard the loud double note of the cuckoo, apparently directly behind me. He was in reality a furlong away. Wordsworth says:

> O blithe New-comer! I have heard, I hear thee and rejoice.
>
> O Cuckoo! shall I call thee Bird, Or but a wandering Voice?

While I am lying on the grass

Thy twofold shout I hear,

From hill to hill it seems to pass,

At once far off and near.

Concerning the all too common crimes of shooting, snaring, and eating little singing birds, the English poet, Ralph Hodgson, has expressed himself in words that ought to be everywhere read

I saw with open eyes Singing birds sweet Sold in the shops

For the people to eat, Sold in the shops of Stupidity Street.

I saw in a vision

The worm in the wheat
And in the shops nothing
For people to eat:
Nothing for sale in Stupidity Street.

CHRIST OR CAESAR

"Our country! In her intercourse with foreign nations may she always be in the right; but our country, right or wrong." "My son! may he succeed in business honestly; but honestly or dishonestly, may he succeed." "My college! may she win all her football games fairly; but fairly or foully, may she win."

I

TODAY the Religion of Nationalism is the most widespread and the most powerful religion in the world. The War of 1914-1918, instead of strengthening the spirit of internationalism and the brotherhood of man, gave an immense impetus to nationalistic fervour. Today Europe is filled with assertive and selfconscious states, and these states are filled with men and boys who will eagerly throw away their lives to obtain or preserve a certain name for their locality. Under any name the citizens would be able to work, play, marry and have children, and go about their daily affairs; but they will gladly kill or die to decide whether their country shall be called a Something or Something-else. If any one doubts whether or not the nationalistic spirit is strong in Asia, all one has to do is to look at India, where men are dying daily for what seems to them a sacred and holy cause.

In time of war, the average father is glad to have his son at the front; proud to sacrifice him for his country. The Gold Star mothers are the Saints of Nationalism. Many modern readers deride the Bible story of Abraham and Isaac; they think it abominable that Abraham consented to sacrifice his son for his religion. If he had revolted and said that his own son was dearer to him than his religious faith, he would seem to many modern readers an admirable character. But the very men who most loudly condemn the ethics of that story are the first to sacrifice their own sons for the religion of Nationalism.

There is not a single country in the world today, big or little, which would not instantly send all its healthy young men into the shambles of battle, if the political party which happened to be in control of the government should decide on a declaration of war. Furthermore, it is probable that the majority of these young men would be glad to go, eager to enlist; no other religion, historical or contemporary, can show such universal devotion, such unreserved willingness to die for its tenets.

In comparison, the Christian religion, widespread as it is, has only a minority of adherents, and only a minority of these would give their lives for the faith. Perhaps the most powerful influence in every country is that of the reigning social class. What is "the thing" to do? There is here no comparison possible between the social standing of Nationalism and of Christianity. Imagine if you can a state of things where as many fathers and mothers would be as proud to have their sons foreign missionaries as they are now proud to have them soldiers. In nineteen centuries there has been an enormous rise in the social respectability of the Christian Church; but it by no means has yet reached the social elevation of a military record in time of war.

The destruction of life has always seemed more glamorous than its preservation. An unselfish scientist, traveling into dark regions infested with disease and danger, traveling there for the sole purpose of saving human life, has little glory in comparison with leaders of armies, who travel there for the purpose of destroying as many human lives as possible.

The physician has never had the appeal or the magnetism of the soldier. Not long ago I heard Doctor Charles-Edward Amory Winslow of Yale University give an eloquent address on the vast number of lives saved by the scientific men who had driven out yellow fever and other pestilential diseases. But in the large audience attentively listening, I do not believe there were three men who could have given the name of a single one of these gallant saviours. In Hartford there is a statue erected in honour of the physician who played an important part in the discovery of anesthetics; he was of course one of humanity's greatest benefactors. Not long ago,

I was talking with the famous musician, Ossip Gabrilowitsch. He had been in Hartford the day before, and said he had seen this statue in Bushnell Park, but had forgotten the name. "Oh," said I, "that is a statue in honour of the physician who made an independent discovery of anesthetics." "What's his name?" "Well, now, I can't quite remember whether it is Wells or Welch." Mr. Gabrilowitsch burst out laughing. "Isn't it ridiculous? we don't either of us know the name of this great man, but I am sure we could repeat the name of every prominent general in the Civil War." As it is certain that the majority of those who read this page are as ignorant as we were, I will set down here that the name of this man of genius was Horace Wells. I looked it up in an encyclopaedia.

II

WAR has behind it several thousand years of glory. The Old Testament, the poems of Homer and Virgil, the literature of the whole world, have exalted the renown and splendour of armed men. Fighting is an animal instinct, though only human beings have organized it. It is as fundamental in man as is any other powerful instinct, like hunger, lust of the flesh and the lust of fame. But civilization, reduced to its final expression, means simply the control of human instincts. Civilization is a slow process. We must not expect a speedy cessation of war. It may be many centuries before the world sees the dawn of universal peace.

The evil of war brings out the virtue of courage. Whatever we may think of war, we do well to honour individual heroes. On every Memorial Day, even those of us who like myself regard war as a relic of barbarism, as incompatible both with Christianity and with civilization, do well to celebrate the courage of those who died in battle. We are not glorifying war. We are remembering brave men who sacrificed their lives. We humbly and loyally give them our tribute of praise.

What should be the attitude of a Christian minister in time of war? He is a good citizen and a good churchman. He is a patriot and he is a follower of Jesus Christ. His position is a difficult one. It is quite natural, therefore, and what might have been expected, that during the World War some ministers were pacifists and some were exactly the opposite. Men who are hostile to the Christian religion find any stick good enough with which to beat a Christian minister. Therefore, some ministers were attacked for "disloyalty" and some attacked for patriotism. Curiously enough, it was the enemies of Christianity, not its adherents, who attacked those parsons who did not condemn the war.

Now I think something is to be said for these Christian ministers. Although I do not like to see a church turned into a recruiting station, although I do not like to see Caesar usurping the throne of Christ, it must be remembered that Christian ministers as a class are not loafers. They are workers. They are men with disciplined bodies and disciplined minds. If a large group of men, women and children should decide to migrate beyond the frontier, as happened often in the early days of our country, and attempt to settle down in a wilderness, the hardest workers would be the ministers. They do not stand aside and watch the labour of others. In the World War, when nearly every one (women as well as men) was "doing his bit," it seemed intolerable to many Christian ministers to sit in the seat of the scornful; to condemn the energy of these earnest people; to take a superior ethical standpoint, from which to view all the workers. This willingness to co-operate, especially strong in a time of desperation, analogous to the exciting job of putting out a fire, helps to explain, I think, why so many ministers assisted their country in the hour of peril.

Naturally, there were various mental attitudes among those who "helped to win the war." The old hymn says, *Faith of our fathers! we will love Both friend and foe in all our strife; And preach thee, too, as love knows how, By kindly words and virtuous life.*

There were ministers who displayed no hatred to the official enemy; they gave their own efforts to the Red Cross, they took part in the various "drives" for money; they did their best, not their worst. In order to show the extremes taken by certain Christian ministers, I will cite two cases. There was a Baptist minister in New York who howled execrations at the

Germans in a manner worthy of the imprecatory Psalms, and who from the pulpit called pacifists "damned cowards."

And there was a Baptist minister in Vermont, who because he conscientiously could not support war, spoke against it from the pulpit. He was arrested, tried, condemned, and sent to prison for fifteen years.

III

CONSIDER the source and the standards of the Christian religion, both of which are to be found in the New Testament. It was Barabbas and not Jesus who was the bad citizen, the agitator. Jesus never attacked the government. The Gospels and the Epistles show no hatred of Rome. Quite the contrary. "Render therefore unto Caesar the things which are Caesar's; and unto God the things which are God's." St. Peter in the Epistle said, "Fear God. Honour the king." The Christian is to be a good citizen, as in general he certainly ought to be. But toward the end of the first century, how different is the attitude! Then the Christian could not be patriotic, could not be a "good" citizen. In the Book of the Revelation, the government is anathema. Why?

Jesus had not concerned himself with politics. His kingdom was not of this world. But in the book of the Acts of the Apostles we find that Luke is anxious to prove Paul's political orthodoxy, and to insist he was not seditious. Furthermore, the Roman officials are represented as admirable men-honest, impartial, tolerant. Repeatedly they saved the life of the great apostle. It is clear from the Epistles that St. Paul believed in good citizenship, and in obedience to civil law.

In the Apocalypse the Christian had to choose between Nationalism and Christianity. And because he put the Christian religion first, he suffered; but his faith triumphed and survived. The security of the Christian Church today has been bought at a fearful price. So long as a Christian had merely to pay tribute money to Caesar, the Christians did not object. But when, toward the end of the century, the attempt was made to force every one to worship the Emperor as a divine being, the Christians revolted. We surely regard Daniel as a hero because he refused to recant his religion, though ordered to do so by the State. Well, the Christians toward the end of the first century refused to worship Caesar.

In Russia today they refuse to worship Lenin. Do American Christians think Russian Christians should put Nationalistic Atheism, the official religion of the Russian government, ahead of their own faith? In the days of the French Revolution, when Christianity was abolished by law and another religion substituted by the official government, what was the duty of Christians?

When in America the Mexican War was in progress, James

Russell Lowell attacked it on the ground that war was incompatible with Christianity.

Ez fer war, I call it murder, There you hev it plain an' flat; I don't want to go no furder Than my Testyment fer that; God hez sed so plump an' fairly, It's ez long ez it is broad, An' you've gut to git up airly Ef you want to take in God. Lowell added in a note,

The attentive reader will doubtless have perceived in the foregoing poem an allusion to that pernicious sentiment, "Our country, right or wrong." It is an abuse of language to call a certain portion of land, much more, certain personages, elevated for the time being to high station, our country. I would not sever nor loosen a single one of those ties by which we are united to the spot of our birth, nor diminish by a title the respect due to the Magistrate. . . . We are inhabitants of two worlds, and owe a double, but not a divided, allegiance. In virtue of our clay, this little ball of earth exacts a certain loyalty of us, while, in our capacity as spirits, we are admitted citizens of an invincible and holier fatherland. There is a patriotism of the soul whose claim absolves us from our other and terrene fealty. Our true country is that ideal realm which we represent to ourselves under the names of religion, duty, and the like.

These words were written not by an enthusiast or by a visionary, but by a man of genius who later served his country in high and responsible stations. They are noble words; but we should remember that when saying them Lowell was supported by local public sentiment in New England, where the war was unpopular. It is probable that when Lowell uncompromisingly called war the same as murder, and incompatible with the teachings of Jesus, he sincerely supposed he would never support a war. Yet when the Civil War broke out, Lowell did not call it murder, but supported it with all his power.

During our Spanish War, "Mr. Dooley" ridiculed the undertaking, and the late Professor William Graham Sumner delivered a public lecture called "The Conquest of the United States by Spain." In the Boer War, G. K. Chesterton, Lloyd George, John Morley, Campbell-Bannerman, and other public men attacked the government o£ their country. In all these instances, conscience triumphed over Nationalism.

IV

ONE of our leading theologians, Professor Douglas Clyde Macintosh, a Canadian by birth, wishes to become a citizen of the United States, but wishes also to reserve the right whether or not to support this country in the event of war, saying he must follow his conscience rather than his possible obligations as a citizen. The judges in the Connecticut Court refused him citizenship, interpreting the law to mean that a foreign candidate must support his adopted country without any reservations. This seemed unfortunate, not for Professor

Macintosh, but for the United States; men of high education, of noble character, of sensitive conscience, are best fitted for citizenship, most needed by every country. Yet the law is the law, and it seemed that the Professor had no case at all.

But he appealed; and the higher court in New York, with a unanimous decision of the three judges, admitted the candidate, stating that the Constitution of the United States never intended to interfere with the inalienable rights of conscience. judge Manton said, "They are given by God, and cannot be encroached upon by human authority without. criminal disobedience to the precepts of natural as well as revealed religion." This is a very important decision.

Some years ago when Madame Schwimmer carried a somewhat similar case to the United States Supreme Court, she was denied citizenship, but a dissenting opinion was written by Oliver Wendell Holmes, who said, *Some of her answers might excite popular prejudice, but if there is any principle of the Constitution that more imperatively calls for attachment than any other it is the principle of free thought -not free thought for those who agree with us but freedom for the thought that we hate. I think that we should adhere to that principle with regard to admission into, as well as to life within this country. And recurring to the opinion that bars this applicant's way, I would suggest that the Quakers have done their share to make the country what it is, that many citizens agree with the applicant's belief and that I had not supposed hitherto that we regretted our inability to expel them because they believe more than some of us do in the teachings of the Sermon on the Mount.*

The supreme value of these tests-and perhaps that is why Professor Macintosh insisted, at considerable mental anguish, on appealing his case-is that here the teachings of Christ come squarely and uncompromisingly into conflict with the Religion of Nationalism. When he was forced to choose, the Professor decided he would rather be a Christian than a citizen. He is a Christian first and an American second. Is not that the right order for every true Catholic and every true Protestant?

I believe that in the future the Catholic Church, the best organized form of the Christian religion, will do much toward the abolishment of war. During the World War, George Bernard Shaw declared that if he were the Pope, he would without hesitation immediately excommunicate every Catholic soldier in every country who did not lay down his arms. Well, it is as difficult to imagine what Mr. Shaw would do if he were Pope, as it is to imagine him holding that august office. But his remark emphasized the international nature of the Organized Church.

It certainly seems tragic that in the late war English Catholics gladly butchered Austrian Catholics; and that German

Catholics gladly butchered American Catholics. I wonder if the powerful and well-organized Catholic Church Universal will always endure such a state of things?

The fact that such a state of things seemed both inevitable and natural is a proof of the tremendous strength of the Religion of Nationalism. It triumphs over every other bond that unites men. Science, the love of truth, all political organizations, were as powerless against it as was the Church. Socialists in all countries were butchering Socialists in other countries. French research scholars in science were gladly engaged in butchering research scholars of the "enemy." The love of truth was eclipsed by sentimental Nationalism. There were certainly more Christian ministers, however, who sacrificed themselves for the truth than there were scientists. Most of the scientists were engaged in devising more powerful engines of destruction. I can think of only one man of science who put what he regarded as the truth above the emotion of nationalism-Bertrand Russell.

V

PATRIOTISM is a noble and beautiful sentiment, as noble and beautiful as loyalty to one's family. In ordinary circumstances, that is to say in times of peace, can there be any doubt that Christians as a rule are the best citizens? They are the best citizens as they are the best sons, husbands, and fathers. Both country and family receive the devotion of religious men and women. The members of the Church of Christ are law-abiding; they are not criminals. They do their public duty, they individually contribute to the support of the nation, they are for the most part, honest, intelligent, up right, the salt of the earth.

Now although they love their families and their homes, would they cheat, lie, steal or murder in order to help or preserve their families? and would they be praised if they did? They would not. Their religion comes first, their families second.

In America the Fourth of July and the Twenty-fifth of December are both legal holidays. There has been within the last fifty years an elevation in the average mental attitude toward both these days of jubilation. The standard of patriotism and the standard of religion have both risen. Although our age is the age of noise, on one day of the year-the Fourth of July-there is less noise than formerly. We show our patriotism today in a diminishment of gunpowder and in a diminishment of oratory. When I was a boy, there was in every town and village in America a "Fourth of July oration," which the patient populace felt compelled to hear. The muzzle velocity of the orator of the day was tremendous; he roared at the top of his lungs, celebrating with voice and gesture the past, the present, the future of the "greatest nation on the face of the earth." This speaker was chosen not because he had anything to say, but because he excelled his rivals in the ability to maintain a fortissimo.

Well, we have changed all that. Such an oration today would be received either with derisive laughter or with a steadily decreasing number of listeners. This does not mean that we are less patriotic than previous generations; it means that our love of country is not to be measured by rhetorical violence. Furthermore, so many boys (and innocent bystanders) were maimed, blinded, and killed by the indiscriminate use of gunpowder (exclusively for patriotic purposes) that city governments finally came to the conclusion that the display of patriotism must take a more sensible form. Let us hope that the catch-word, a "safe and sane Fourth" may eventually mean a safe and sane mental attitude in all loyalties.

True patriotism, sincere love of one's country ought always and everywhere to be shown not by boastful jingoism, but by manners and conduct that display good breeding. One of the definitions of patriotism in Webster's Dictionary is devotion to the welfare of one's country.

I should like to see all Americans, instead of being proud of having the greatest wealth in the world, or the most powerful navy in the world, or the best climate in the world- I should like to see them proud of belonging to the most unselfish country in the world, the most generous country in the world.

I think it is true that Americans are the most amiable of all people, the most good-natured, the most jolly; but I should like to see the word American stand not merely for good-nature, but for good behaviour, for modesty, for kindness, for tolerance, for breadth of mind and culture. We should compete with other countries not in armaments or in riches, but in the fruits of the Spirit.

A man who is truly ambitious does not wish to excel his neighbours in physical strength or in truculence; he does not hope that his neighbours will be afraid of him; he wants them to like him, to admire him, to respect him, to love him, to come to him as to an intimate friend. The same thing applies to one's country. A loyal and patriotic American does not have to wave the flag or beat the drum. He does not wish to have other countries afraid of the United States, to look upon us with distrust, suspicion, and hatred. He wants his country so to behave in the eyes of the world that we shall be the most loved and admired of all nations; that our actions will be better than our words; that we shall always be expected to do the right thing because we are Americans. Whatever sacrifices are involved in gaining the love and respect and confidence of other countries are certainly judiciously made. We cannot afford to insist on the legal pound of flesh at the price of hatred.

VI

Now as there has been an improvement in the significance of the word patriotism and it is certain that in the future the word will reach a still higher elevation, so the connotation of the word religion has of late years been enriched and ennobled. Religion has come to be not primarily an affair of the voice, but of the life. The Master invariably stressed character. Speaking exclusively to his professed disciples, he said, "Why call ye me Lord, Lord, and do not the things which I say?" "Not every one that saith unto me Lord, Lord, shall enter the Kingdom of Heaven; but he that doeth the will of my Father who is in Heaven." Men and women are judged by their lives. The only convincing answer to atheism and scepticizm is to live like a Christian. This is more difficult than to argue with, or to denounce, or to ridicule the atheist; but it is also more effective.

In the same way, the professions of a nation are judged simply and wholly by its conduct. If the official voice of a country proclaims the love of peace and good will and charity and affection for all the nations of the earth, and at the same moment the same country is building up a navy with the intention of having the biggest and most powerful armament in the world, this official voice will be regarded as the voice of a liar. It would really be better not to make any pretty speeches; it would, indeed, be better to speak the truth.

In most nations today the word anarchist has a bad odour; but from the point of view of international law, at this moment every nation in the world is an anarchist. An anarchist is one who believes in absolute individual freedom; who recognizes no law except his own desire. Well, not long ago when it was reported that Japan had made some statement that might be taken as derogatory to the United States, our Senate went on record as declaring that the United States of America could not tolerate any interference or suggestions from any other nation. It is probable that in this very year of grace nothing would be more hotly resented by the majority of our accredited political representatives than a remonstrance or even advice from any other country. What is that but international anarchy?

When a new region is first invaded by settlers, every man is a law unto himself; and every man goes armed. After a time, such a condition of things becomes intolerable; individual license forbids community liberty. Vigilance committees are formed; and in process of time, a central government is established.

All those who insist with such vigour that the United States must on no account enter into any alliance with other nations are really insisting that every nation should be and remain an anarchist. Fortunately, they are also resisting the Time-Spirit. They are imbedded in the superstitions of the past and are blind to the future. They are looking in the wrong direction.

For it is as certain as anything can be that our American descendants will live in a World League.

VII

PROFESSOR ROBERT MILLIKAN, one of the foremost physicists of the world, says in his book Science and the New Civilization that there are three leading ideas in the world of thought and science. First, foremost, and of the highest importance, he puts the Golden Rule. He believes this Law to be more important than the law of gravitation or than the principle of evolution. It is the profoundest truth known to man. The greatest teacher in history not only said "Love thy neighbour as thyself," but in response to the question, "Who is my neighbour?" he left no doubt that our neighbours were all the children of men. The fact that a man lives on the other side of a national boundary line does not cancel his neighbourship, or release us from our neighbourly duty.

Live and let live. Prejudice is an ugly thing and Tolerance a fine thing; but there is something more splendid than tolerance. It is Fellowship.

The actual realization that all the world is one family is the ideal for the true patriot. If the words Fatherhood of God and Brotherhood of Man have any meaning whatever, if they are anything except hypocritical cant, then there can be no such thing as a foreign war. Every war is a civil war.

But not only is international friendship desirable, it has become a necessity. War simply won't do. As the murder of another man's body is the suicide of the murderer's soul, so one nation cannot with spiritual safety destroy another.

The first Fourth of July celebration was in a war. The most "glorious Fourth" in the future will be that one which celebrates, in the language of the poet, The Parliament of Man, the Federation of the World.

VIII

WE CANNOT have the Millennium now, but we can do our best to improve present conditions. For every country at this moment to abolish its army and navy would be as absurd as it would be to abolish courts of law or prisons. Tolstoy, who, like most Russians, was an extremist, insisted on the abolishment of law courts and policemen. But what sensible Christian, remembering the Boston police strike, would advocate that? We are not living, not yet, in Paradise; we must do the best we can in this imperfect world.

Even the most thorough-going idealist must recognize facts-the actual, existing conditions. Aylmer Maude, in the new Centenary Edition of the Works of Tolstoy, writes, Tolstoy stated the case against patriotism and war powerfully, and it was important to have this well done in order to have some literary counterpoise to the patriotic influence exerted by the classics and the Old Testament-books written when people did not know other nations, but sincerely hated them, and when the foreigner was a natural enemy and men believed that their national God abhorred the "Gentiles," and desired to see the Hivites and the Amorites smitten hip and thigh.

Tolstoy showed convincingly that Christianity, with its doctrine of the Fatherhood of God, is fatal to patriotism, and that even those who object to the word "God" and prefer some other phraseology, can frame no rational outlook on life which justifies the sacrifices the modern world offers up on the altar of international jealousy and enmity sacrifices often as reckless and as blind as those that of old were offered to Moloch or to Mars.

What he did not see, however, was the rational basis that exists for national feeling of a non-malevolent kind. If the world is to be organized, law to prevail, and Governments to rest on the will of the people (all things of which we generally approve), then it is practically necessary that the world should be subdivided into kingdoms of manageable proportion, and once such subdivisions exist, it is natural to remember that "charity begins at home," and our first duty is to see that we get things rightly arranged in our own section....

However horrible war may be-and I regard it as on a par with slavery, duelling, and cannibalism-to stop it by the method

Tolstoy commends (that of each conscientious man refusing to serve as a soldier or to pay taxes) has the grave disadvantage that if successful it would disintegrate the State, and if attempted by all humane people, would throw the control of affairs into the hands of those who were not humane.

Life is full of perplexities. The relation of a loyal Christian to his country in the next war is not easy to predict; because no one can read the future. No one knows when the next war will come, or what kind of war it will be. Therefore I myself, as a Christian and a patriot, will refuse to say now that in the future I would never under any circumstances support a war; for I do not know but that I might be forced to choose between two evils. In the Civil War many Quakers fought against slavery. If in this world we could choose only between black and white, how easy our choice would be! But it was Hegel, I believe, who said that in most cases we are forced to choose between Light Brown and Dark Brown; and if we believe, of two courses, that one is fifty-one per cent right, then perhaps that course deserves one hundred per cent of our support. But in all cases I would put the religion of Christ first and everything else second.

IX

IT is often said that people in the Twentieth Century have lost the sense of sin. But Christians who know that their lives are spent in a daily fight against sin, rejoice that in one respect the world has reached a consciousness of sin hitherto not only unfelt, but for the majority of people, unknown.

There is everywhere a growing sentiment that war is sinful. In the Middle Ages, the Christian organizations rejoiced in the slaughter of heathen, the butchery of infidels; they believed their chances for eternal salvation increased in direct proportion to the number of unbelievers they had personally extinguished. In the American Revolution, although some Americans were patriotic rebels and some were patriotic Tories, apparently none believed there was in war itself anything wicked or inconsistent with fervent piety. The same conditions of public opinion existed in our Civil War. Northern orthodox ministers rejoiced whenever Southern church-members were killed; they saw no incongruity between preaching the gospel of Jesus and endeavouring to carry on the war against their brethren in the South. They did everything possible to increase the strength of the fighting spirit in the North. Northern Episcopal clergymen were delighted when that Southern pillar of the church, Bishop Leonidas Polk, was killed in battle.

The standards of the Christian religion have not fallen but risen. During the World War there were not only many Christians who refused to fight under any circumstances, there were thousands engaged in the struggle who constantly felt its incompatibility with the religion they professed, and "carried on" merely to make the best of a bad job. This sentiment has been markedly increased by the books that have multiplied since the war. Any book or any drama today which represented war as sentimentally glorious, would receive almost universal ridicule.

X

MANY enemies of Christianity have declared that the World War destroyed the Christian religion. The Christian prestige was certainly injured by it, as it ought to have been. Many lost their faith. Faith is always dimmed by anything that works against the conception of Triumphant Goodness. But so far from the Christian religion having been destroyed by the late war, I believe it is the other way around. In the long run, it is War and not Christianity which will get the worst of it. Long after war has ceased to be, men will continue to build churches, to read the Gospels, to say their prayers. The personality of Jesus will dominate mankind in the distant future more powerfully than at any period in the past.

Every true Christian is looking fearlessly and confidently forward. We hope not only that America will join other nations in the reduction of armaments, we hope she will lead the way. We should assist every move in the direction of peace; we should take a prominent part in every movement to bring together as in one family all the nations of the earth. The peace-makers are not ridiculous; there is no greater folly than war.

Those who maintain it is hopeless to stop war, that war always has existed and always will exist, are narrow conservatives, devoid of progressive spirit. The same courage and spirit of co-operation that have been employed in the prosecution of war, will some day be employed in attaining and in maintaining peace.

When Thoreau was addressing an audience, he exclaimed, "There's a good time coming, boys!" A certain heckler sneered, "Can you fix the date?" Thoreau replied, "Will you help it along?"

XI

YES, there is a good time coming, "though a battle's to fight ere the guerdon be gained, the reward of it all."

I see unmistakable signs of the coming conflict between the religion of Christ and the religion of Nationalism. The world today is conscious as never before of the sin of war, of its incompatibility with religion, with civilization, with intelligence, with the pursuit of learning, with every true conception of the brotherhood of man.

When this conflict comes- and it is surely coming- then it will cost something to be a Christian, as it did in the first century. The chief difficulty with the Christian Church today is that it means so little. In order that it may rise to its possibilities- for if all Christian church-members united now, war could be prevented- it may be necessary in the future for Christians once more to become unpopular, as they were in the ancient days of persecution, as they were in France in the eighteenth century, as they are now in Russia. The strength of the religion of Nationalism is shown by the willingness of its followers to sacrifice their lives. If the religion of Christ is to become lusty, it must receive not merely a polite and passive acquiescence, it must demand and receive the supreme sacrifice.

I feel that the Christian Church is once more to be tested. Instead of church membership being a comfortable social asset, it is going to hurt. Then the Christian Church will suffer from persecution and become strong; thousands will leave it as rats leave a sinking ship. They leave it because they are rats. Perhaps it was sinking because it carried too many rats. Perhaps it will sail more buoyantly after the rats have left it.

If there is one thing of which I am certain, it is the ultimate triumph of the principles of the Christian religion. Already it has one great advantage over the religion of Nationalism. The religion of Nationalism is compulsory; those who do not give it first place are forced to do so. But compulsion has never in the long run succeeded.

The religion of Christ is voluntary. Many men and women, many teachers and college professors, any businessman may refuse his allegiance or even defy it with impunity and with security. No citizen is compelled to go to church. The Christian Church is made up wholly of volunteers; there are no drafted men. In this lies its potential strength.

The time is coming when the promise of the First Christmas will be abundantly fulfilled. Then every Christmas will be more than a family celebration, more than a legal national holiday; it will be the realization of peace on earth and good will to men.

THE END

CIRCUS

HEAVEN lay about me in my infancy, and it tools a circular shape. From the moment I entered the great tent until I emerged some hours later I was in Paradise. It was no illusion, no imaginary pleasure. It was authentic bliss, a delirium of delight. And now that I am over 70 I find I still love the circus. I do not go today for the pleasure of reminiscence, to see if I can recapture my childish enthusiasm; I go because the circus draws me, because I want to go.

I have always loved the circus. When I was a child, although my father and mother did not allow me to attend the theatre, they heartily approved of the circus and I remember seeing repeatedly not only Barnum's Greatest Show on Earth, but Barnum himself. During a pause in the circus performance, P. T. Barnum, dressed in formal black clothes and looking like a clergyman, was introduced to the audience as one of the greatest benefactors of mankind, which I do not think was an exaggeration. He was broad and fat and unctuous and in the language of Dickens, he seemed to be "one vast substantial mile." I wish I could remember what he said, but I was so fascinated by looking at the author and creator of happiness that I do not recall a single word of his brief address.

Barnum was the Shakespeare of advertisers, and has never keen surpassed. His knowledge of what the public wanted was infallible. He knew they loved to be swindled, so long as the swindle was understood to be a glorious joke on both sides. At one of his circuses he had a big sign just inside the main tent

TO THE EGRESS

Hundreds of people followed that thinking they were on the way to some African monstrosity, but soon they found they were outdoors and had to pay fifty cents to get back. Instead of being wild with rage, they were delighted and when the word was explained to them they said, "Isn't that just like Barnum !"

On another occasion in New Haven one of the side shows, to which I believe an admission of twenty-five cents was charged, announced

A CHERRY COLORED CAT Now people supposed that a cherry colored cat was unique; they trooped in there by the hundreds and all they saw was a perfectly ordinary black cat. When they had looked at this and demanded an explanation, the attendant said "Well, you know some cherries are black." And then what happened was exactly what Barnum had foreseen. Instead of being angry, the crowd looked at each other with a foolish grin, exclaimed "Sold again !" Then they went back into the main tent and told every stranger "Have you seen the cherry colored cat? It is the most marvelous exhibition ever given." So that each person who had been deceived got five other persons to swell the coffers of the management.

In this particular instance I not only remember the occasion but I had a personal acquaintance with the cat. The cat lived at the corner of Chapel and York Streets in New Haven in a large house belonging to Mrs. Sanford. I had often stroked and petted this cat. Two or three days before Barnum's circus came to town the cat disappeared. The day after the circus had left, the cat returned to the house with a ribbon and card on which was inscribed "Mr. Barnum's compliments."

Times have changed since then but the circus remains in all its splendor and magnificence. I remember when I was a child the three hours from two o'clock until five o'clock in the afternoon in the big tent were to me absolutely undiluted bliss. I was in an ecstasy of enjoyment. It is certain that if I am fortunate enough to enter the real and eternal Paradise, nothing in Heaven will give me more superlative, immaculate joy than those three hours in the circus.

After I grew up, while I put away many childish things, I did not put away the circus. I know there are many people who never attend the circus after they grow up, and there are others who go merely to take their children. Now while I have often taken children to the circus in later years, I do not take them merely so that I may see the circus through their eyes or enjoy it through their minds. I go to the circus because I want to, because I love it and always will love it. I like everything about the circus-the international smell, the peanuts, the pink lemonade, the sawdust, the animals, and the amazing gymnastic feats are as thrilling to me as ever.

There is a certain so-called disillusion element in the circus which is, I believe, a fallacy. When we are children we envy all the acrobats and performers; we think they must lead the most wonderful lives; they are our heroes and heroines; they are our idols, and then when we grow up we are told that their lives are really very unhappy, very miserable, and that they are not really to be envied at all. Now this statement, so constantly repeated by older people to children, is not true. It is the exact opposite of true. The performers in the circus enjoy their work enormously; they would not have any other profession or occupation for anything in the world. Their loyalty to their profession and their interest in the circus are so great that when one of the acrobats becomes disabled through an accident, he always hopes that he may be given a job as a ticket taker, or that he may be retained in some capacity so that he may spend all the rest of his life in association with the circus. Thus, our pessimistic friends who attempt to disillusionize childhood, are themselves completely mistaken.

The circus is one of the greatest institutions in the whole world. It makes an enormous contribution to human happiness. I congratulate John Ringling North, its executive head; Henry Ringling North, his brother, and the other members of the Ringling family who are now carrying on the great tradition in a way fully worthy of all the advances made in modern times.

CITY AND COUNTRY

It is generally assumed that the country is more romantic, more poetical than the city; but it would not be so easy to prove this, if one were put to the test. "God made the country and man made the town," said William Cowper, which meant simply that he preferred rural life.

It is rather amusing to consider that in our age, which is so often called the age of machines, and when many people are afraid that simplicity and individuality will be lost, country places, mountain scenery, and the wilderness are more popular than ever before.

Now there are fashions in outdoor nature just as there are fashions in clothes. Today every-one must profess a love for mountains whether one really likes them or not; for mountains are very fashionable. Switzerland is the play-ground of the world; and the inhabitants make a larger income off their barren rocks than most communities make off fertile and productive plains.

But it is only within two hundred years that mountains have been generally admired. Before that time they were usually regarded as ugly excrescences, both disagreeable and dangerous; and at the best they were no more to be regarded as objects of beauty than pimples.

English gentlemen who made the Grand Tour in the seventeenth century thought the Alps were disgusting; they were a monstrous and abominable barrier that must be crossed before the traveller could reach the smiling landscape of Italy.

When Addison wrote home from his travels in 1701, he said that he had had "a very trouble-some journey over the Alps. My head is still giddy with mountains and precipices; and you can't imagine how much I am pleased with the sight of a plain!"

Such a remark would injure the reputation of a modern pilgrim; but Addison made it in perfect good faith, and with no apology.

Perhaps some of our contemporary love of wild scenery is owing to the comfortable circumstances in which we behold it; transportation, tunnels, fine hotels, luxuries of every description enable us to view mountains in security and serenity; but if we had to pass over them in acute discomfort and in constant danger, our attitude might be more like Addison's. This by no means explains why the once "horrid" has become fashionable; but it helps to explain the modern love of wild scenery.

Had Addison been told that two centuries later people would build hotels on the edge of Alpine precipices, he would have dismissed the idea as a silly dream; no one would put a road-house there. "But, Mr. Addison, I am not talk ing of roadhouses. These hotels are not on the way to something else; they are not a means, they are an end. People will travel three thousand miles from California to New York, sail three thousand miles from New York to Europe just to spend the summer in a mountain hotel, where it costs twenty dollars a day-" he would have regarded the coming generation as idiotic.

It was Thomas Gray, author of the *Elegy*, who was one of the first English travellers to see the beauty of the Alps, and it was he therefore who is originally responsible for making them fash-ionable. He and Horace Walpole drove over the mountains in a chaise, and Gray wrote to his friend West, "Not a precipice, not a torrent, not a cliff, but is pregnant with religion and poetry.

There are certain scenes that would awe an atheist into belief." This was a new note in literature.

It is my belief that mountains and wild scenery are more appreciated today by citified folk who love them for the change and novelty than they are by those who are forced to live among them all the time. When I was young, I walked with three of my college mates from New Haven to the White Mountains; it was a fine expedition, and took us some three weeks. I remember toward twilight on a certain day we entered a gorge and passed through into a place surrounded by austere mountains.

A farmer addressed us: "Where do you boys come from?"

"Connecticut."

He slowly and solemnly repeated the word CONN-ECT-ICUT-as though he were saying MESOPOTAMIA, and added, "My, I'd like to see Connecticut."

We told him it was not so very remark-able. "We have no such mountains as these in Con-necticut." He replied, "Oh, damn these mountains! I'm sick of the sight of them." And it appeared that he had never been out of that valley.

I spend a quarter of my life in the country, and love it, but if I had to choose between living all my life in the country or in a large city, I should choose the city immediately. And I believe this is true of most people.

A crowd of unemployed some years ago stood in line at the Detroit city hall. A man came up and offered every one in turn good wages, good food, a good place to sleep, and plenty of fresh air, if he would take for the summer a job on a farm. Every one of the men laughed at him.

Some of us more fortunate folks are irritated by this, for in America everybody thinks that every body else ought to be a farmer. But the truth is that man does not live by bread alone. People do not live in order to live-merely for healthy surroundings and good food. They want excitement, they want something interesting.

Who can blame them? Don't you feel that way yourself ?

We should all contribute to the Fresh Air Funds, because little children of the slums ought to have a chance to see unimpaired nature. But very few of the children would be willing to stay there, and in some cases after a few days they are homesick for their native filth. The city is one continuous theatre, admission free; the street is the best playground in this world. There is a fire, a street fight, the appearance of policemen,

an arrest, an automobile accident-all the day and all the night, "something doing."

Thus it is not at all strange that the majority prefer the crowded conditions of the slums to the fresh air of the country; for other things being equal, isn't that about the way we all feel?

DREAMS

I look upon horrible dreams as one of the assets of humanity, one of the good things of life; because one feels so elated after waking. I am convinced that most men and women do not sufficiently appreciate the advantages they possess. They either exaggerate their sufferings and drawbacks or, instead of enjoying what they have, they spend their time in longing for what is beyond their reach.

Just as it takes an illness to make one appreciate the satisfactions of health, so one needs a calamity to make one realise how good daily existence really is. It is often said that experience is the best teacher. This is by no means always or even often true. Experience charges too much for her lessons.

There is no good in learning how one might have shown sagacity in business after one is bankrupt; there is no good in discovering how one ought to have avoided a certain article of diet after one is fatally poisoned; there is no good in receiving the proof of the danger in carelessly driving a motor car after one lies dead in the ditch.

Now the best way to discover how cheerful daily life may be is to be visited by a frightful dream. The horrible wild beast has seized us, because when we tried to flee, our legs were lead.

Just as it is about to sink its terrible tusks in our shrinking frame, we wake up, and hear the good old trolley car go by. Hurrah! it was only a dream; and we are alive on the blessed earth. And we have learned how sweet plain ordinary life is without the lesson costing us anything but a transitory sweat.

I think, too, that many who either profess to hate life or at all events refuse to admit anything good about it, might appreciate it more if they could be temporarily transferred, not to hell; but to their own imagined heaven. Wagner in the famous music-drama, *Tannhauser*, has given an admirable illustration. This knight, like all his fellow-creatures, felt the call of the senses; he was transported from this imperfect earth to the pagan Heaven, where he lived in the constant society of Venus. But after a time this palled upon him and eventually became intolerable. He tore himself away, and suddenly found himself back on the earth. He was in a green pasture in the springtime, and a shepherd boy was singing-what happiness! The accomplished German dramatist Ludwig Fulda wrote a play, *Schlaraffenland.* There was a poor boy, ragged, cold and chronically hungry. He dreamed he was in a magic land. Remarkable birds flew so slowly by him that he found he could reach out his hand and grasp them. He did this, and lo, he had in his hand a broiled chicken! He ate several with avidity. but could not eat forever. Glancing at his ragged garments, a wardrobe door flew wide, and he had his choice among many elegant suits. Thus every desire was instantly and abundantly gratified. After some time, this palled upon him, and then became so unendurable that he gave a yell of horror; he woke up. He was cold, ragged, and hungry; but his heart was singing. He was back on the good old earth.

Thus, whether we dream of hell or of heaven, it is usually with a sigh or even a shout of satisfaction that we find ourselves back on this imperfect globe.

Many persons tell me that they never dream; their sleep is blank. It is with me quite otherwise; I almost always dream; many of my dreams are extraordinarily vivid and some are unforgettable.

When I was a child I dreamed three nights in succession of the Devil. The first night the Devil chased me upstairs. I ran as fast as I could, but sank down when only half way up. Then the Devil took from his pocket a shoemaker's awl and bored it deftly into my right knee. The second night the Devil was in my front yard. Suddenly he changed into the form of a dog; and when another dog rushed barking at him the satanic hound swallowed him as easily as one takes a pill. The third night I also dreamed of the Devil, but I have forgotten the details.

One of the worst dreams I had in childhood was when I was being attacked by wild beasts, and suddenly my mother appeared on the scene. I shrieked to her for help, and she looked at me with calm indifference. That was the worst dream I ever had, and you may be sure it went by contraries.

I suppose the only way we can distinguish dreams from what is called actual life is that in dreams the law of causation is suspended. There is no order in events, and no principle of sufficient reason to account for them. Things change in an impossible manner. Apart from this, dreams are as real as life while they last.

I often have prolonged dreams that are not only fully as real as waking experiences, but are orderly and sensible, and sometimes delightful. Many years ago I dreamed that I was walking the streets of a Russian city with Count Tolstoi. It was one of the most agreeable and most inspiring days of my life, and I have always regretted it never happened. We walked together for hours and discussed modern literature. He said a great many wise and brilliant things, all of which I have, alas, forgotten. The only feature of that dream unlike reality was that Tolstoi had shaved off his beard.

Wilkie Collins, in *Armadale,* suggested that every dream we have is a repetition of an experience that has actually happened to us during the preceding twenty-four hours. I read that novel in my boyhood and was impressed by that explanation of dreams, and for several months I wrote clown my dreams and found that every one was suggested by something that had happened to me during the preceding day.

The only thing I am certain of in dreams is that they do not in any way forecast the future. When I was a child I dreamed I saw heaven and Jesus sitting on a cloud. He called to me, "Willie Phelps, come here." The next day I told my father and mother about it, and to my surprise they were exceedingly alarmed.

ENGLISH AND AMERICAN HUMOUR

Some one has said that American humour consists in overstatement and English humour in understatement. This judgment does not include everything, but so far as it goes it is not only accurate, but helps both to explain English humour and the frequently heard remark that the English are without it. I suppose one reason many ill-informed Americans say that Englishmen have no sense of humour is because the English do not indulge so commonly as we in boisterous jocularity, exaggeration, surprise and burlesque. The average Englishman does not see why a stranger should accost him with jocosity-many Englishmen do not see why a stranger should accost them at all. It is an excellent plan while travelling in England or anywhere in Europe never to speak first to an Englishman; let him open the conversation.

One of the chief differences between the average Englishman and American is in amiability, responsiveness, amenity. Americans are probably the most amiable people in the world, the most happy to respond to an exploratory remark, the most willing. I dare say it is partly a matter of climate. Our chronic sunshine makes us expansive and ebullient.

In any American city on a terrifically hot day, two hitherto unacquainted men will speak to each other as they pass on the street, one saying, "Don't you wish you had brought your overcoat!" which harmless jest is returned by the other with equal affability. If you said that to an Englishman, he might stare at you blankly, and perhaps hazard the query, "You mean, of course, your light overcoat?"

After introduction to a resident Englishman in Vancouver, British Columbia, at a small dining-table in a hotel, I remarked gently, "Even though you are behind the times here in Vancouver, I do not see why you should advertise the fact." "What on earth do you mean?" he enquired. Then I called his attention to the dinner-card, on which was printed Vancouver, B. C. He exclaimed, "But it doesn't mean that, you know!" I do not believe he was deficient in a sense of humour. I had just met him, and he did not see why a stranger should be sufficiently intimate to be taken otherwise than seriously.

Punch is the best of comic papers; it expresses the genuine original humour of a humorous folk. I remember seeing there a picture of the village orchestra, and as the director rapped for attention, the first violin leaned forward and asked, "What is the next piece?" and being informed, replied, "Why I just played that one."

Woodrow Wilson once told me a story which illustrates how dangerous it is for anyone to assume that the English have no sense of humour.

Three Americans were telling anecdotes to illustrate the English dearth of humour, when they saw approaching a representative of that nation. It was agreed that he should then and there be put to the test. So one of them stopped him and narrated a side-splitting yarn. The Englishman received the climax with an impassive face. The American, delighted, cried, "Cheer up, old man, you'll laugh at that next summer." "No," said the Briton, gravely, "I think not." "Why not?" "Because I laughed at that last summer."

The humour of English political campaign speeches at its best, is unsurpassed. When the late John Morley had finished an oration by requesting his hearers to vote for him, one man jumped up and shouted angrily, "I'd rather vote for the devil." "Quite so," returned the unruffled statesman; "but in case your friend declines to run, may I not then count upon your support?"

A perfect retort was made to the great and genial Thackeray, on the one occasion when he ran for Parliament. He met his opponent, Edward Cardwell, during the course of the campaign, and after a pleasant exchange of civilities, Thackeray remarked, "Well, I hope it will be a good fight, and may the best man win." "Oh, I hope not," said Cardwell.

The English are the only people who seem to be amused by attacks on their country; does this show a sense of superiority that increases the rage of the critic? Or is it that their sense of humour extends even to that most sacred of all modern religions, the religion of nationalism?

The Irish are supposed to excel the English in humour; but it is a fact that English audiences in the theatre are diverted by sarcastic attacks on the English, whereas it is physically dangerous to try a similar method on an Irish audience. The Irish patriot, Katharine Tynan, said that if she could only once succeed in enraging the English, she would feel that something might be accomplished. "But," said she, "I tell them at dinner parties the most outrageous things that are said against their country, and they all roar with laughter." Undue sensitiveness to attack betrays a feeling of insecurity.

Typical American humour is not subtle and ironical; it is made up largely of exaggeration and surprise-Mark Twain was a master of ending a sentence with something unexpected. "I admire the serene assurance of those who have religious faith. It is wonderful to observe the calm confidence of a Christian with four aces." Anthony Hope, in his recent book *Memories and Notes,* says that when Mark made his first dinner speech in London before a distinguished audience, there was intense curiosity as to what he would say. He began with an unusually slow drawl. "Homer is dead, Shakespeare is dead and I am far from well."

Another true story (which I took pains to verify) happened during the early days of his married life, which synchronised with the beginnings of the telephone. Incredible as it may seem, Mrs. Clemens had not heard Mark swear, for during the engagement he had managed by superhuman efforts to refrain from what he called that noble art, and she did not dream of his oral efficiency. But one day, thinking he was alone, he started to use the telephone. (The Paris Figaro says that to get your telephone connexion is not an achievement; it is a career.) Mark, having difficulties, poured out a torrent of river profanity. He looked around and there was his wife, frozen with horror.

But she had heard that the way to cure a husband of profanity was for the wife to swear in his presence. So, in a cold, artificial voice, she said, "Blankety-Blank-Blank." Mark cried, "Darling, you know the words, but you don't know the tune!"

Mark had a way of combining philosophy and humour. This is the gospel according to Mark Twain. "Live so that when you die even the undertaker will be sorry."

GOING ABROAD THE FIRST TIME

There is no thrill like the first thrill. When Wilhelm Meister kissed the Countess, Goethe said they tasted "the topmost sparkling foam on the freshly poured cup of love," and Goethe knew what he was talking about. I shall always be glad that my first trip to Europe had three features-I was young; the steamer was small; we landed at Antwerp.

I was twenty-five and in perfect health; my head was stuffed with literature, descriptions and pictures shrieking for verification; my mates and I rode bicycles across Europe and over the Alps; we lived with impunity in cheap inns and on cheap food; we were soaked to the skin by frequent rains; we were exposed to every inclemency of the air and to innumerable germs in rooms, food and water; we were never sick. We stored away memories which have been paying daily dividends.

It is not well to wait until one is old, for an American is, as a rule, never physically comfort able in Europe. Unless one is reeking with cash one is almost always chilly or damp or hungry or filled with the wrong kind of food. But Europe has all the things an intelligent American wants to see, and it is best to see them when one's health is rugged enough to rise above inconveniences.

I am glad I went on a small boat, for I asked a traveller who recently returned on an enormous ship if the sea was rough: "I have no idea, I never saw it." Our little *Waesland* had only one deck, and that was sometimes awash. It was not a hotel, it was a ship. Finally, instead of landing at Cherbourg at some unearthly hour, being transferred to a squeaky lighter, and then to a train with long hours of travel before one reached the destination, we steamed up the Scheldt past the windmills and stepped off the boat right in the midst of one of the most interesting cities in the world. The transition from America to Europe was as dramatic as it could possibly be, unshaded by tenders and trains. Thus I advise first-timers to sail either to London or to Antwerp; you embark at New York and you disembark at the desired haven.

I love Europe, London, Paris, Munich, Florence, with inexpressible fervour; but I can never recapture the first careless rapture. I remember after that fine first afternoon and evening in Antwerp, when we walked about in ecstasy in the rain, we bicycled to Bonn from Cologne, and that evening before going to bed in the little Rhenish inn, I looked out from my bedroom window on the river and on the roofs of the quaint old town, and I said, "Is it real or is it a dream?"

The next day was a fulfillinent; for when my classmate, George Pettee, and I were sophomores, we were sitting in the top gallery of the theatre watching a picture of the Rhineland put on the screen by John L. Stoddard. One of us turned to the other and whispered: "I'll shake hands with you on standing on that spot within seven years." The answer was, "You're on! We had no money and no prospect of getting any; but in five years, not seven, we stood on that identical spot, and as we leaned our bicycles up against the road wall, we reminded each other of the night in the gallery. It is pleasant to dream; but it is pleasanter to make the dream come true.

The most beautiful country I have ever seen is England. It has not the majesty of Switzerland, but it has everything else. Almost exactly the same size as North Carolina or Michigan, it has an amazing variety of scenery and climate. As one approaches it from the Atlantic, the cliffs of Cornwall look austere and forbidding; but there the roses bloom in January. Stand almost anywhere in Devonshire, and you see the meadows leaning on the sky; they are separated from one another not by stone fences, or by split-rails or barbed wire, but by hedgerows in self-conscious bloom; Salisbury Plain is like Western Nebraska, a far horizon; the misty slopes of the Sussex downs reach dreamily to the sea. Every few miles in England the topography changes; could anything be more different than those different counties?

But we do not go to England for natural scenery, though we might well do so; we go because in England every scene is, in the phrase of Henry James, "peopled with recognitions." The things that we have seen in imagination we see in reality; there they are! The September afternoon when I bicycled alone to Stoke Poges and saw the churchyard in the twilight exactly as it was in 1750 when Gray described it, I fell on my knees. As we looked from the top of the hill down into Canterbury, the setting sun glorified the Cathedral; as we stood on the most solemn promontory in England, Land's End, and gazed into the yeasty waves at the foot of the cliff, I remembered Tennyson's lines:

One showed an iron coast and angry waves. You seemed to hear them climb and fall And roar rock-thwarted under bellowing caves, Beneath the windy wall.

And here one of the Wesley brothers wrote the familiar hymn about the narrow neck of land and the divided seas.

One day, talking with an Englishman on the train, I raved about Warwickshire and about Devon. "Ah," said he, "if you haven't seen the valley of the Wye you haven't seen England." Accordingly, we went to the little town of Ross in the West; there we hired a rowboat, and two stalwart sons of Britain rowed us many miles down the stream. Occasionally, the river was so shallow they poled us over the pebbly bottom; sometimes it was so narrow we could almost touch the shores; then it would widen out nobly, and we saw the white-faced

Hereford cattle feeding in green pastures. "What castle is that?" I asked, pointing to a ruin on a hill. "That is Goodrich Castle, sir." And that is where Wordsworth met the little girl who knew her departed brother and sister were alive.

We moved by Monmouth, sacred to Henry V, the Roosevelt of kings; we came to Tintern Abbey, and you may be sure we stopped there; whatever you see, don't miss the valley of the Wye.

HAPPINESS

No MATTER WHAT may be one's nationality, sex, age, philosophy, or religion, everyone wishes either to become or to remain happy. Hence definitions of happiness are interesting. One of the best was given in my Senior year at college by President Timothy Dwight: "The happiest person is the person who thinks the most interesting thoughts."

This definition places happiness where it belongs-within and not without. The principle of happiness should be like the principle of virtue; it should not be dependent on things, but be a part of personality. Suppose you went to a member of a State Legislature, and offered him five hundred dollars to vote for a certain bill. Suppose he kicked you out of his office. Does that prove he is virtuous? No; it proves you can't buy him for five hundred. Suppose you went to the same man a month later and offered him a million dollars-that is, instead of making him a present, you make him and his family independent for life, for the best thing about having money is that if you have it, you don't have to think about it. Suppose, after listening to this offer, he should hesitate. That would mean he was already damned.

He is not only not virtuous, he knows nothing about virtue. Why? Because his virtue is dependent not on any interior standard, but on the size of the temptation. If the temptation is slight, he can resist; if alluring his soul is in danger. Such virtue is like being brave when there is no danger, generous when you have nothing to give, cheerful when all is well, polite when you are courteously treated.

Fortunately there are in every State Legislature some men who have no price, who are never for sale, who look upon all bribes with equal scorn-and these are the virtuous men. After the same order, there are boys who are just as safe in Paris as in Binghamton; just as safe at three o'clock in the morning as at three o'clock in the afternoon; just as safe with evil companions as with good companions. Why? Because these boys do not allow place, time, and people to determine their conduct, they attend to that matter themselves. Their standards are within.

So far as it is possible-it is not always possible-happiness should be like virtue. It should be kept or lost, not by exterior circumstances, but by an inner standard of life. Yet some readers of this page will lose their happiness before next Sunday, though I hope they recover it. But why lose it, even for a season? There are people who carry their happiness as a foolish woman carries a purse of money in her hand while walking on a crowded thoroughfare. The first man who is quick with his fingers, nimble with his feet, and untrammelled by conscience, can and will take the purse away, and disappear with it. He will have separated the woman and her money. Now if one's happiness is like that, an exterior thing, dependent on an enemy's volition, on a chance disaster, on an ill wind, on any one of a thousand accidents to which we are all exposed-then happiness can be lost.

All of us have enemies. I regard myself as on the whole an amiable person, and yet there are a considerable number of people, who, when they hear of my death, will feel relieved. I care as little about that fact now as I shall then. I do not intend to let other people, especially those who do not like me anyhow, determine whether I shall have peace of mind or not. If some one reports to you a malicious word that someone else has said of you, and in consequence of that, you become unhappy, you have allowed another person to hold the key of your heart, to settle whether you shall be happy or not. I insist that you ought to determine that question for yourself. Instead of being angry or distressed when people hate you, suppose you regard it as amusing; for if you are honestly trying to do your best, and incur hatred for your pains, there is about such a situation something funny. If you can appreciate the humour of it, you are free.

It is impossible for anyone to feel every moment exuberantly happy; to feel, on rising from bed every morning, like a young dog released from a chain. If you felt that way chronically, you would become an intolerable nuisance; you would get on everybody's nerves. But I am certain that with the correct philosophy, it is possible to have within one's personality sources of happiness that cannot permanently be destroyed. You will have days and nights of anguish, caused by ill-health, or worry, or losses, or the death of friends; but you will not remain in the Slough of Despond; you will rise above depression and disaster, because you will have within your mind the invincible happiness that comes from thinking interesting thoughts.

If the happiest person is the person who thinks the most interesting thoughts, then the mind is more important than either of those tremendous blessings, wealth and health. I never indulge in slighting remarks about money, because if I did, I should be a hypocrite. Money is a blessing; I should be glad to distribute a large sum to every one of my readers, of course reserving the usual commission. But money is not the chief factor in happiness. If it were, then everyone who had money would be happy and everyone without it would be unhappy; but there are so many wealthy people who are unhappy and so many poor people who are cheerful, that money, however important or desirable, is not the determining cause. It would be folly to speak slightingly of health. No one realises what a blessing health is until one has lost it; then one has to devote time and energy and money to recovering it. Anyone who is careless of his health is a traitor; because one's usefulness, one's capacity to do good in the world, is usually seriously lessened by poor health. Yet even health is not the sine qua non. People without it think they would be perfectly happy if they were well. A man with a toothache imagines that everyone in the world without a toothache is happy-but it is not so. There are healthy people who are not happy; and there are invalids whose faces, eyes, and conversation reveal an inner source of happiness that enables them to triumph over bodily ills. They have overcome the world, the flesh, and the devil.

I should be sorry to lose what money I have, but unfortunate as it might be, such a loss would not permanently destroy my happiness. I should be sorry to be run over by an automobile, and lose my right leg; but such a loss would not permanently destroy my happiness. Why not? Because my happiness is centred neither in my purse nor in my leg; but in my mind, my personality. The Irish dramatist, St. John Ervine, lost a leg in the war. I asked him which he would prefer, to have two sound and healthy legs again, and not be able to write novels and plays, or to be as he is now, with only one leg, but an accomplished man of letters? He did not hesitate. He said there was no comparison possible; he would far rather be a one-legged writer, than a two-legged something else. "And yet," he murmured thoughtfully, "I do miss that leg."

There is another important consideration. If the happiest person is the person who thinks the most interesting thoughts, then we grow happier as we grow older.

Of course I know that such a statement runs counter to the generally expressed opinion. The majority of novels and poems and the common gossip of society assume that youth is the golden time of life.

> Yet ah! that Spring should vanish with the rose!
>
> That youth's sweet-scented manuscript should close!
>
> The nightingale that in the branches sang
>
> flh, whence and whither flown again, who knows?

When I was an undergraduate, a distinguished man addressed us, and he said emphatically, "Young gentlemen, make the most of these four years; for they are the happiest years you will ever know." The remark was given to us with that impressiveness that so often accompanies a falsehood. For it was a falsehood.. My classmates and I have been out of college forty years; most of us are happier now than then.

I read many French novels, and I often see a woman of forty-five described as a "woman for whom life was over." Over at forty-five? and why? Because strange men do not stare at her. Doubtless it is sweet to be admired, doubtless flirtation is one of the normal pleasures of youth, doubtless it is agreeable to be regarded as a pretty animal; but is that all there is in life for a woman? One cannot penetrate below the surface of such a statement without finding an insult to personality.

No one should make a statement like "youth is the happiest time of life" without being prepared to accept its intellectual consequences. If it were really true that youth is the happiest time of life, nothing would be a more tragic spectacle than college boys and young maidens; for they would in their present state have attained the pinnacle, the climax of existence; before them lie fifty years of diminuendo, of decay, of accumulating loss, of descent into ever darkening days.

Some middle-aged silly women become romantically sad as they talk about what they are pleased to call their lost youth; I maintain that it is as absurd for a woman of fifty to mourn because she is no longer twenty as it would be for a woman of twenty to sob because she is no longer three. And indeed there are some idiots who declare that childhood is the happiest time of life. "Ah, that I were a child again!" Don't worry; you soon will be.

The belief that youth is the happiest time of life is founded on a fallacy-on a false definition of happiness. Many people think that to be free from physical pain and mental worry is perfection; knowing that as we grow older our physical pains and mental worries are apt to increase, they assume that youth is the happiest time of life. We are, of course, all animals; but we ought not to be merely animal. I suppose that in the case of animals, youth is the happiest time of life; a puppy is happier than an old rheumatic hound; a young jackass braying in the pasture is presumably happier than an old donkey laboriously drawing a cart; but these are merely animals, and lack man's greatest gift the possibility of development.

Those who say that childhood is the happiest time are unconsciously postulating the animal definition; a child is happiest because he is healthy and has no worries; when he is cold, somebody covers him; when he is hungry, somebody feeds him; when he is sleepy, somebody puts him to bed. Yes, but when he is not sleepy somebody puts him to bed. There is the shadow on the sunny years; there is the fly in the ointment. Personally I had rather have a few worries and aches, and go to bed when I choose. A child is as dependent as a slave. If you would rather be a healthy, welled slave than an independent man, you will prefer childhood to maturity. A child is at the mercy of adults both physically and mentally. They are stronger than he and can force him to do what they wish; they are cleverer than he, and can invariably outwit him. Let me give an illustration of both.

When I was six years old, I was playing ball with a contemporary. It was my ball, my property; that is to say, father had given it to me. Well, I made a muff, the ball rolled into the street, and a bigger boy grabbed it. "Here," I shouted, "give me that back.

That's my ball."

"'Tain't yours now," said he,

with a disagreeable grin, "I've got it"

"No, but it don't belong to you, it's mine!"

"It ain't yours any longer," he rejoined, and he was correct. It wasn't. He has got it still. I never saw it again. All I could do was to sit down and cry. Do I want to be a child again?

At about the same age, I was fortunate enough to own a silver three cent piece. And in those days, one could really buy something for three cents. Not wishing to spend so large a sum at once, I decided to have it changed. I walked into a large grocery store, and asked the clerk to change my three cent piece. He looked at my insignificant figure and said curtly, "We haven't any change in the store," I withdrew and stood on the sidewalk. A fat Irishman came along and glancing at me, inquired what was the matter.

"The matter, Sir, is that I have a three cent piece and can't get it changed."

"Why don't you go into the store ?"

"They have no change in the store, Sir."

"How do you know that?" "They told me so, Sir."

"Sonny, you come along with me."

I put my tiny hand into the enormous paw of that Irishman, and we walked together into the store, and as luck would have it, we confronted exactly the same clerk who had informed me that there was no change. The Irishman said sharply, "This boy wants his three cent piece changed."

To my absolute amazement, the clerk said civilly, "Why, certainly," opened a drawer, and gave me three coppers. It was one of the first great surprises of my life. Upon reflection, I perceived that if you had no influence, there was no change; the fact was variable, depending simply upon the individual's power to command influence. Today I have both change and influence, and do not care to be a child again.

Happiness is not altogether a matter of luck. It is dependent on certain conditions. One should prepare for happiness as an athlete prepares for a contest. Leave out the things that injure, cultivate the things that strengthen, and good results follow. It is important to grow old successfully, for everyone must either grow old or die; and although the pessimists tell us that life is not worth living, I observe that most individuals hang on as long as they can. It is sad to see so many men and women afraid of growing old. They are in bondage to fear. Many of them, when they find the first grey hair, are alarmed. Now one really ought not to be alarmed when one's hair turns grey; if it turned green or blue, then one ought to see a doctor. But when it turns grey, that simply means there is so much grey matter in the skull there is no longer room for it; it comes out and discolours the hair. Don't be ashamed of your grey hair; wear it proudly, like a flag. You are fortunate, in a world of so many vicissitudes, to have lived long enough to earn it.

There are some foolish people who say, "Well, I mean to grow old gracefully." It is impossible; it can't be done. Let us admit it, because it is true; old people are not graceful. Grace belongs to youth and is its chief charm. The poet Browning hints that youth has beauty and grace because youth would be intolerable without it. Young people are decorative; that is why we like them. They are slender, agile, fair and graceful, because nobody could stand them if they were otherwise. It would be horrible if boys and girls, knowing as little as they do, were also bald, grey-headed, fat, wrinkled, and double-chinned; then they would be unendurable. But Nature has so arranged matters that young people are physically attractive until they acquire some brains and sense, and are able to live by their wits; then they lose these superficial advantages. As responsibility grows, beauty and grace depart. The child sits on your knee, and reaches for your watch. You smile, and say, "Nice baby, can't have de watch!" But when he is thirty and reaches for your watch, you put him in jail. More is expected of us, more is demanded of us, as we grow older; nothing is more tragic therefore than a woman of mature years with the mind of a child. There is in civilised society no place for her.

But even if it were possible to grow old gracefully, it would be at best a form of resignation, a

surrender; and a soldier of life should not take it lying down. Instead of growing old gracefully, suppose we grow old eagerly, grow old triumphantly. Is this possible? With the right mind and character, with the right attitude, with the right preparation, it is not only possible, it is probable. Joseph Ii. Choate was no deluded enthusiast; he was a hard-headed man of the world. When he was past seventy, in a public address in New York he maintained that the happiest time of life was between seventy and eighty years of age; "and I advise you all to hurry up and get there as soon as you can."

Let us examine another fallacy. It is said that as we grow older, we lose our illusions. Of course we do. I do not believe I have a single illusion left; if I have, I would gladly lose it today. For what happens when you lose an illusion?

Every time you lose an illusion, you gain a new idea. Ideas are more interesting, hence pleasuregiving, than illusions. The world as it is, men and women as they are, are more worth knowing than fancy pictures created by ignorance and inexperience. We are told that youth is happy because youth looks on the world through rosecoloured spectacles. But I have no desire to look at the world through rose-coloured spectacles, and I can prove that you haven't. That repository of wisdom and experience, Robert Browning, at the age of seventy-seven, wrote

> Friend, did you need an optic glass,
>
> Which were your choice? If lens to drape
>
> In ruby, emerald, chrysopras, Each object-or reveal its shape Clear outlined, past escape,
>
> The naked very thing?-so clear That, when you had the chance to gaze,
>
> You found its inmost self appear Through outer seeming-truth ablaze,
>
> Not falsehood's fancy-haze?

This can very easily be determined by our old friend in political economy, the law of supply and demand. Demand fixes the price; a thing in great demand is worth more than something for which the demand is feeble. Suppose you were going to Europe this summer, and stopped in at the optician's to buy a pair of powerful binoculars. Suppose he should suggest that instead of getting that, you took a kaleidoscope, where instead of looking at distant objects, you saw pretty rosettes, bright combinations of coloured glass. "Do you think I am a child, to be amused with rose-coloured toys?" "Ah, but distance lends enchantment to the view; when you see a ship five miles away, she is as beautiful as a swan. But if you look at her with binoculars, you see shreds and patches, washing hanging on the deck-lines, and other realities. Surely you don't want the truth."

Surely you do. And the proof is that anyone can buy rose - coloured glasses cheaply, but every time you increase the power of the lens, that is every time you bring reality nearer, the price goes up enormously. If then we are willing to pay cash to substitute truth for illusion, let us be done with saying that youth is happy because of illusion. As we grow older, our eyes become achromatic; rose - colours fall away, and we see life more nearly as it is, and find it more interesting.

It is also often said that as we grow older, we lose our enthusiasms. This need not be true; it is never true with right-minded individuals. There is a fallacy lurking in such a statement. The fallacy is this; we confound the loss of the object that aroused our enthusiasm with the loss of enthusiasm, a very different thing. Things that excite children often fail to arouse mature men and women-which is not a sign that maturity has lost sensitiveness to excitement; it may have lost interest in childish things. When I was a child, the happiest day in the year was the Fourth of July. It was not illusory happiness; it was real; it was authentic bliss. Its cause? On the Fourth of July my mother allowed me to rise at midnight, go out on the street and yell till daybreak. Think of it, I, who usually was forced to retire at eight, was out on a city street at three in the morning, shrieking and yelling! It was delirious joy. Now suppose you should tell me that tomorrow I may rise at midnight and yell till daybreak. I decline.

Does that mean I have lost my happiness, or my enthusiasm? No; it means that I don't care to rise at midnight. During the daytime of the glorious Fourth, I used to shoot off firecrackers hour after hour, with undiminished zeal. Every now and then, I would see a very old man, about thirty-two, come along, and I would offer him an opportunity to share my delight. He always declined. "Poor fellow!" I reflected, "Life is over for him. He has lost his happiness." It never occurred to me that people over thirty had any fun. I supposed they had to go through the routine of life, but had no pleasure in it.

The fact that a girl of three is enchanted by the gift of a doll, and the same girl at seventeen insulted by it, does not mean that the girl at seventeen has lost either her happiness or her enthusiasm; but that the enthusiasm, formerly aroused by dolls, is now stimulated by something else.

If the happiest person is the person who thinks the most interesting thoughts, we are bound to grow happier as we advance in years, because our minds have more and more interesting thoughts. A well-ordered life is like climbing a tower; the view half way up is better than the view from the base, and it steadily becomes finer as the horizon expands. Herein lies the real value of education. Advanced education may or may not make men and women more efficient; but it enriches personality, increases the wealth of the mind, and hence brings happiness. It is the finest insurance against old age, against the growth of physical disability, of the lack and loss of animal delights. No matter how many there may be in our family, no matter how many friends we may have, we are in a certain sense forced to lead a lonely life, because we have all the days of our existence to live with ourselves. How essential it is then, to acquire some intellectual or artistic tastes, in order to furnish the mind, to be able to live inside a mind with attractive and interesting pictures on the walls! It is better to be an interesting personality than to be an efficient machine. Many go to destruction by the alcoholic route because they cannot endure themselves; the moment they are left alone with their empty minds, they seek for stimulant, for something to make them forget the waste places. Others rush off to the motion-pictures, run anywhere, always seeking something to make them forget themselves.

Higher education, the cultivation of the mind, is more important for women than for men; because women are more often left alone. A large part of masculine activity is merely physical; men run around like dogs. But a woman, even in these emancipated days, is forced to be alone more than man. Now take the instance of a girl who has been brought up happily in a large family, with plenty of neighbours and friends, whose bright days pass in happy activities and recreations; she is married to a suburbanite in New Jersey. Every morning he takes the 7.37 train to New York, and

does not return till the 6.48 in the evening. The young wife, rudely transplanted from a cheerful home, is placed in an empty house, in a town where she knows no one, and is alone all day. God help her if she has no mental interests, no ideas, no interesting thoughts

I have no desire to underestimate the worth of physical comfort, or the charm of youth; but if happiness truly consisted in physical ease and freedom from care, then the happiest individual would not be either a man or a woman. It would be, I think, an American cow. American cows and American dogs are ladies and gentlemen

of leisure; in Europe they hitch them up and make them draw loads. Take therefore an average day in the life of an American cow, and we shall see that it is not far from the commonly accepted ideal of human happiness. The cow rises in the morning and with one flick of her tail, her toilet is completed for the whole day. This is a distinct advantage over humanity. It takes the average woman (and it ought to) about threequarters of an hour every single day to arrange her appearance. When Harriet Martineau was a child, she was appalled by the prospect of having to brush her teeth every day of her life. She lived to be ninety. The cow does not have to brush her teeth; the cow does not have to bob her hair; the cow does not have to select appropriate and expensive garments; or carry a compact; one flick, and she is ready. And when she is ready, breakfast is ready. She does not have to light the kitchen fire herself, or to mourn because the cook has left without notice. The grass is her cereal breakfast and the dew thereupon is the cream. After eating for an hour or so, she gazes meditatively into the middle distance querying first, whether that grass yonder is lusher and greener than this, and second, if it be so, whether peradventure it is worth the trouble to walk there and take it.

Such an idea as that will occupy the mind of a cow for three hours. After grazing, without haste and without rest, she reaches by noon the edge of a stream. "Lo, here is water; what hinders me from descending and slaking my thirst?" She descends about waist deep into the cooling stream; and after external and internal refreshment, she walks with dignity to the shade of a spreading tree, and sits down calmly in the shadow. There and then she begins to chew the cud. Her upper jaw remains stationary, while the lower revolves in a kind of solemn rapture; there is on her placid features no pale cast of thought; the cow chewing the cud has very much the expression of a healthy American girl chewing gum. I never see one without thinking of the other. The eyes of a cow are so beautiful that Homer gave them to the Queen of Heaven, because he could not think of any other eyes so large, so lustrous, so liquid, and so untroubled. Cows are never perturbed by introspection or by worry. There are no agnostic cows; no Fundamentalist or Modernist cows; cows do not worry about the income tax or the league of nations; a cow does not lie awake at night wondering if her son is going to the devil in some distant city. Cows have none of the thoughts that inflict upon humanity distress and torture. I have observed many cows, and there is in their beautiful eyes no perplexity; their serene faces betray no apprehension or alarm; they are never even bored. They have found some happy via media by which they escape from Schopenhauer's dilemma, who insisted that man had only the vain choice between the suffering of unsatisfied desire and the languor of ennui.

Well, since the daily life of an American cow is ,exactly the existence held up to us as ideal - physical comfort with no pains and no worries, who wouldn't be a cow? Very few human beings would be willing to change into cows, which must mean only one thing. Life, with all its sorrows, cares, perplexities, and heartbreaks, is more interesting than bovine placidity, hence more desirable. The more interesting it is, the happier it is. And the happiest person is the person who thinks the most interesting thoughts.

HUMAN NATURE

WHEN I WAS EIGHT years old and was spending a week-end visiting my Aunt Libby Linsley, at her home in Stratford on the Housatonic, a middle-aged man called one evening, and after a polite skirmish with my aunt, he devoted his attention to me. At that time I happened to be excited about boats, and the visitor discussed the subject in a way that seemed to me particularly interesting. After he left, I spoke of him with enthusiasm. What a man! And how tremendously interested in boats! My aunt informed me he was a New York lawyer; that he cared nothing whatever about boatstook not the slightest interest in the subject. "But why then did he talk all the time about boats?" "Because he is a gentleman. He saw you were interested in boats, and he talked about the things he knew would interest and please you. He made himself agreeable." I never forgot my aunt's remark.

Like many boys of my time, I learned about religion and morality from my mother, and about etiquette, clothes, and the ways of the world from my aunt. For some reason virgin aunts were always more worldly minded than mothers.

On this occasion Aunt Libby made clear the difference between a gentleman and a bore. A gentleman puts his companions or guests or casual acquaintances at their ease; he is considerate; he has tact; he draws out the contents of the other man's mind, and thus enables him to appear at his best. A bore talks only about the things that interest him himself; he has little perception of the impression he is making, or of the actual state of mind of his victim.

Perhaps the final test of a gentleman is his attitude toward children. I wonder if all men remember as vividly as I do the occasions when grownup people treated us neither with contempt nor with indifference nor with what is worse, grinning condescension-I' And how is my little man today?"-but with unassumed respect. The few occasions in my child-hood when strangers treated me with courtesy produced an indelible impression.

In conversation, the time and the place and the subject should harmonise. There are talkers who have a positive genius for the inopportune.

Not so many years ago, as I was leaving my house to walk to the Yale-Harvard football game, I met a man I knew only slightly, who insisted on discussing literature all the way to the arena of combat. There were the streets crowded with an excited throng, all-except my friend thinking of only one thing; in the midst of this joyous, laughing, noisy multitude, this man wished to know what I thought of the contemporary condition of American poetry.

The relative importance of poetry and football had nothing to do with the occasion. As humour is out of place at a funeral, so a discussion of literature is out of place at the great game of the year. A man's soul is of more importance than a trivial engagement; but if a zealous evangelist stops a man running to catch a train to enquire about his salvation, it is probable he will miss both.

A famous German philosopher, Lotze, who had more influence on the life and character of the late Lord Haldane than any other teacher, defined existence as follows: *To be is to be in relations.* That is to say, a living thing is living because it is in relations, in connexion with something. A dead body is dead because it has ceased to hold any relation to any other thing in the universe. Hence, the more interests a man has the more he is alive. It is unfortunate for boys and girls in school and college if their friends are confined to persons of similar taste, "who talk the same language." Such restriction is still more unfortunate for men and women in society. Every one ought to be on intimate terms with every kind of human being. Theodore Roosevelt was a scholar and a statesman; he had friends in all groups and classes, from missionaries to crooks. Gene Tunney was heavy-weight champion boxer of the world; in addition to his friends in sporting circles, he numbers among his intimate associates clergymen, head masters of schools, leaders in business; and also the most famous man of letters and the most famous man of music in the world-Bernard Shaw and Richard Strauss.

Affectation and pretence are almost invariably the sign of a small mind, of a personage who is distinctly minor. Men who have reached the summit of their profession are almost invariably without pose-they are natural and unaffected. They do not smell of their job, and have none of the traditional trappings of the part. When Lockhart first met Robert Browning, he exclaimed, "Why, he isn't in the least like a damned literary man." But when you see a fifth rate minor poet, he is likely to advertise in his hair and in his clothes and in his speech that he is not like ordinary persons-he is forsooth a Bard.

Many actors play a part more earnestly off the stage than on. A conceited actor was once looking with a friend at a portrait of David Garrick, and he remarked: "They say I look more and more like Garrick every day." "Yes," was the answer, "and less and less like him every night." We so readily expect actors on the stage to act like actors instead of like men, that when a truly great actor or actress appears on the boards we are thrilled by *naturalness,* by the absence of conventional mannerisms.

Affectation is founded on fear. It is a species of bluff. The person fears he will be found out. "A little learning is a dangerous thing," said Pope. It makes one too careful. So the social climber has the veneer of good manners, and "watches out" continually, whereas the born aristocrat does not care what anyone thinks. One with a little learning cannot afford to make a mistake and therefore makes many. The true scholar is the first to admit that there is no such thing as human infallibility.

The great poets, novelists, dramatists have as a rule simple and natural manners. Many years ago I spent an evening at his house in Paris with Maurice Maeterlinck. He had published a number of plays that dealt with the uncanny and the supernatural, and I dare say many imagined him to be a pale, dreamy, lackadaisical person. On the contrary, he was absolutely common-sensible, frank, hearty, downright-the best word to describe him would be the word jovial. He offered me a cigarette, and being somewhat rattled, I stuck the lighted end in my mouth, which gave him much innocent mirth.

Bernard Shaw, who with his pen has slain tens of thousands, gives one in conversation the impression of cheerful kindliness. His manner is as free from cynicism as it is from conceit. One feels he would be the best of friends in or out of need. I suppose there is nothing so tiresome to the true hero as hero-worship. Lindbergh literally takes the wings of the morning to escape from it. A hundred years ago a stranger met the Duke of Wellington on the street, and asked if he might shake hands. He then remarked, "Now I will tell my grandchildren this is the hand that shook the hand of the conqueror at Waterloo." The Iron Duke replied, "Oh, don't make a damn fool out of yourself."

There is no doubt the most conceited people in the world are the most obscure-I don't put it the other way around; I don't say the most obscure are the most conceited, for there are plenty of obscure persons who are the salt of the earth. The most erudite scholar measures himself by the highest standards and feels ignorant-the greatest writer, I suppose, knows how far short he is of the ideal, and hence is modest; but the man of small ability and large ambition has no sure basis of comparison and overestimates his production. A man who has never succeeded in getting a single line into print often thinks his verse is as good as Milton's, his plays as good as Shakespeare's, his novels equal to Tolstoi's.

Many manuscripts sent in good faith to every magazine would astound the readers if they were printed.

In the last analysis, human nature is an inexplicable mystery; it is, as the Russians say, a dark forest. Browning spent his whole life as a specialist in human nature, and he was forced to admit that he knew nothing about it. All he could do was to record instances of "queer" behaviour, but he ridiculed those who were cocksure of others' motives, while the great physicians were so often mistaken about bodily symptoms.

"You are sick, that's sure"-they say; "Sick of what?" they disagree. "'Tis the brain"-thinks Doctor A; "'Tis the heart"-holds Doctor B; "The liver-my life I'd lay!"

"The lungs!" "The lights!"

Ah me!

So ignorant of man's whole Of bodily organs plain to see So sage and certain, frank and free, About what's under lock and keyMan's soul!

Those whom we think we know best will often surprise us by not running true to form; no wonder, then, we are often amazed by finding in

strangers some trait absolutely contrary to their facial expression. Eugene O'Neill, in his play *The Great God Brown,* built a powerful drama on the idea that everyone wears a mask. When I was six years old, I learned for the first time the difference between a mask and reality. I was walking up Chapel Street, New Haven, and as I neared the corner of College Street, I saw a very old man, bent over with infirmities, wearing a copious white beard. He kept stopping pedestrians and asked in a broken, pathetic whine, "Won't you give a poor old man a penny?" I looked at him with childish pity. Suddenly he came over to me and whispered "Don't you worry about me! I've got loads of money." He whipped out of his pocket a canvas bag, containing a pint of solid cash. Then he lifted his beard, and behold, he was a smoothshaven young man. He laughed gaily. The next instant he had turned, stopped a passer, and repeated his begging question with tears in his voice. Now why do you suppose he made that revelation to a little boy? Did some impulse force him? Was the expression on my face so sincere that he could not bear to deceive a child, or was it that he could not endure to have me go away sorrowful for one who was so well able to take care of himself? I did not give him away.

Some thirty years later, I stood in line at a railway-ticket-office, and marvelled at the courtesy and deference shown by the ticket-seller to the silly and flustered purchasers. Their questions, it seemed to me, would have ruffled the patience of job. "How much did you say it was? Are you sure the train stops there? Is there no train before the next one?" To all these superfluous enquiries the ticket seller replied with sweet and smiling courtesy, showing no trace of irritation or impatience. When I finally reached him, I quietly complimented him on his steady politeness. He broke out in a stream of profanity. I must have touched a nerve and released a pent-up spring in this apparently patient man.

One reason I have never been able to take a cynical or depreciatory view of the mass of mankind is because I know so many specimens of so many different classes. I do not admire that oft-quoted saying by Carlyle to the effect that the population of the earth is mostly fools. In the first place, I cannot make myself feel that tremendous sense of personal superiority to the average run of mankind which is necessary to complacent cynicism; in the second place, while the history of mankind in general is "whole centuries of folly, noise, and sin," men, women, and children in particular often show noble traits and characteristics.

There are many snobs and selfsatisfied individuals who the moment they enter a crowded trolley car or subway, glare at the other passengers in the firm belief that every one except the glarer is a fool or a knave.

I claim no credit either for human sympathy or for loving-kindness or for democratic sentiment when I say that I could not feel that way if I tried. For I am certain that every person in that crowd has some fine quality; is perhaps at this very moment under appalling difficulties displaying a courage far greater than mine would or could be.

Just as the level of intelligence and morality in a mob may be lower than the lowest member of it-for the rotten apple in the barrel not only degrades the others but steadily itself grows more rotten-so a consideration of humanity in the mass is neither edifying nor cheering; hence it will usually be found that the cynics and the scorners and the haters are *lookers* on.

That is, they are as they are because they are ignorant.

If they knew more individuals from all classes and knew them intimately, their affection and respect for men and women would rise. How often we read in the newspapers or take an oral report of what some man is supposed to have said, and we immediately decide that the man is a fool. Then perhaps later we meet and talk with this very same person, and find he is anything but a foolhe is a man of sense and good judgment. All we needed for the correct understanding of him was a little more knowledge.

In international affairs, it is probable that a complete knowledge by the citizens of one country of the citizens of another country, would make war impossible. In 194, the average Englishman supposed that the average German lieutenant was inhuman, some kind of monster; the soldiers who fought against him knew better. The average German thought Sir Edward Grey-a quiet English gentleman who loved birds-was a dark, designing, smooth, hypocritical villain, plotting with lies and treachery against the peace of Europe. Lichnowsky knew better.

Mr. Gerald Stanley Lee was on the right track when he suggested that millions and millions of dollars be expended by each country to *advertise* its real nature and aims in other countries. Spend at least part of the money now devoted to threats-for every battleship is a threat-on disseminating knowledge. It was a happy idea of the Australians last year to send several hundred Australian boys around the world and have them entertained by the citizens of every town they visited in their separate homes. Why not send the entire House of Commons on a similar journey? It pays to advertise.

The road to sympathy with and affection for human beings lies through knowledge and more knowledge. The British reviewers who ridiculed the poetry of Keats called him Johnny Keats. His brother said "John is no more like Johnny Keats than he is like the Holy Ghost." Our conceptions of other persons are frequently, perhaps commonly, as far from the truth as that. I have just been reading a book of intimate recollections of Gladstone, written by his son, called *After Thirty* Years. He wrote it because every recent biography of his father seemed to the family, who had the best knowledge of him, to present a portrait grotesquely unlike the original.

Now I suppose no biographer except Boswell and the Old Testament writers has succeeded in telling the truth about his hero. Hence Lord Gladstone, instead of writing a biography, put down a succession of anecdotes and instances which show that Gladstone was not in the least like the man set forth in all seriousness by the professional portrait painters.

As we grow older, we are less and less likely to call others insane. Many prominent men have had the weakness to imagine that every one who differs from them is both intellectually inferior and morally delinquent; and there are persons who secretly think that those who hold contrary opinions are at least partially crazy. Tolerance comes with years and experience, because years and experience bring knowledge. Just as two persons talking in Russian seem funny to an American boy, when they are really not funny at all; so there are persons who seem to others insane, simply because the others lack experience. When Browning was twenty-four years old, he published two poems which he called *Madhouse Cells.* One described a theologian who believed in predestination, the other described a lover who murdered the woman of his heart. Later in life, Browning reprinted these poems, but omitted the title. As he grew older and observed how many individualists walk the streets, he became more and more unwilling to call anyone insane. Wise men and women, as they descend into the vale of years, become more and more tolerant, that is, more and more sensible.

Just as a variety of human relations enables one to live more abundantly, so a continuance of alert interest in a variety of subjects enables one to live longer. I mean just exactly what I say. Physically all who have passed forty begin to deteriorate; there is no way to prevent it; although people differ very much in their comparative power of bodily activity. But mentally some men and women never grow old, no matter how many years they have to their credit. If they maintain a constant interest in the world about them they will actually live longer than those whose curiosity diminishes or decays.

I think I can point out the exact moment when a man begins to grow old. It is the moment, when, upon self-examination, he finds that his thoughts and reflexions in solitude turn more to the past than to the future. If a man's mind is more filled with memories and reminiscences than with anticipation, then he is growing old.

This need never be the case. A few weeks ago I called on a gentleman in Boston, who in a few months will be ninety. As I came into his library he was vigorously playing the typewriter. He rose, greeted me cordially, and we had a lively conversation about current affairs.

There are old men and women whose minds are fully as powerful as in the days of their youth; but their minds have lost alertness, resilience; if the conversation continues on a certain theme, they can hold up their end and do their part; but if the theme of talk changes rapidly from this to that, as it so often does, they are left behind. I believe that this loss of mental agility, in the majority of cases, need not happen. One must watch oneself, and not fall a victim either to the garrulity or the egotism of decrepitude. One should always remain a person and never become a personage. My Bostonian changed from one topic to another with the ease and springiness of youth.

Many years ago I was invited by my friend Mr. Richard B. Glaenzer to meet the great French actor Constant Coquelin, who was then playing in New York. It was a large dinner party, and though we all did homage to the guest of honour, there was another man present who aroused in my mind even greater wonder and enthusiasm. He was that magnificent American, John Bigelow, who forty years before, had been American Minister to France. He was now ninety years of age. Never shall I forget him as he appeared on that evening. Long after midnight he sat beside. Coquelin. He was smoking a huge black cigar and chattering French with the great actor, with all the vitality and sparkle of youth. John Bigelow never had time to grow old.. He was too constantly interested in an immense variety of contemporary ideas and things.

John Bigelow was an intellectual athlete; but a continuous and keen interest in life will prevent the advances of age in a bodily athlete. The former prize-fighter, James J. Corbett, is now well over sixty; he is more interesting to meet and talk with than when he was young. His auto biography, *The Roar o f the Crowd,* is a valuable contribution to psychology; for it shows that Corbett has always been as much interested in human nature as if he were a novelist or playwright. Some years ago, I was dining in the Hotel Grunewald in New Orleans, when I saw Mr. Corbett enter at the other end of the room. I said to my table-companion, "That's Jim Corbett!" and the waiter, thinking I had an appointment with him, brought him at once to my table. Well, I found him a more interesting man than the ordinary casual acquaintance; he was interesting because his mind was so quick and agile-what I call a prehensile mind.

The old-fashioned shoe-maker or cobbler was invariably an interesting man; I suppose that his labour being mechanical, he had plenty of time to *think,* which with many busy people has become a lost art. When I was a boy, I had only one pair of shoes at a time; so when these needed to be cobbled, I had to sit an hour or two hours with the shoemaker, while he soled and heeled my shoes. I always found him entertaining. He had meditated and reflected long and deeply, and I reaped the harvest of his solitary hours.

One of the most intelligent men I ever knew could neither read nor write. He was a coast-guardsman in Michigan, a member of a life-saving crew, and his name was Sam Neal.

His long hours on duty at all hours of the day and night were filled with meditations on life and human nature. He had immense common sense, excellent practical judgement, and what he knew he knew thoroughly. He had pondered, sometimes sadly, more often humorously, on various types of men and on human experience. I learned much from him, and it was a delight to hear him talk.

Bernard Shaw, who hates and despises all forms of competitive athletic sports, like football, tennis, golf, etc., says that nearly all men are no better than playboys. That we never grow up. That even when we reach the age of seventy, we are still interested in childish things. This is of course true, but perhaps if we were not interested in sport, we should be no better for the lack of it. Still, to any student of human nature, the enormous place taken by sport in the life of the average man is food for reflexion. During the most exciting period of the World War, I was travelling on a train in Illinois. The morning came, and we were all eager to get the news. Finally a boy appeared, bringing the Chicago morning papers. Sitting next to me was a clergyman, in ecclesiastical uniform. He bought a paper, and without looking at the first page, turned excitedly to the sporting columns and read the chronicles of yesterday's games. Not only do millions of fairly civilised persons read the sporting pages every day, but men who are quite intelligent in other respects, are enormously elated by a victory in golf, and correspondingly depressed by defeat. This emotion is unreasonable. If we were reasonable creatures, we should not particularly care. We should say, '(Oh) it's only a game, and I have had the fresh air, good company, and pleasant recreation." But whoever saw a golf-player who talked or felt like that?

The late Professor William D. Whitney, the former Sanscrit scholar in the world, author of a long list of learned books, member of any number of learned European societies, was finally forbidden by his doctor to play any game, croquet, checkers, cards, or what not, because he suffered such agony when defeated that it had a disastrous effect on his nerves and mental energy.

A prominent banker in a midwestern city was an excellent businessman. He was serious, dignified, and wise. He had the respect of all who knew him; he was a pillar of society. Well, one day he was playing golf for a little recreation. He made a miserable shot with his brassy. He leaped up and down in a transport of rage, broke the club in two, and then bit it with savage fury.

Three friends of mine were playing golf with a famous nerve specialist. On their way through the green and pleasant land, the doctor told the other men that golf was a splendid thing if one did not take it too seriously. "It is a pity," said he, "that men cannot remember that, after all, it is only a game. If they play well, all right; if they play badly, let them not get excited. For if one takes golf too seriously, it does far more harm than good." Shortly after he had completed this homily, the players came to a tee where they had to drive across a lake. The doctor drove into the water. He laughed and drove another ball into the water. This time he did not laugh, but drove a third ball into the water. Then he cursed, threw every one of his clubs into the lake, threw the golf bag after them, and walked loudly away to the clubhouse. Such is life. Such indeed it really is.

There is no study more interesting than the study of human nature. But in order to have even a little knowledge and understanding of this illimitable theme, one must in imagination put oneself in the other man's place. I think one reason why so many people appear stupid or silly or crazy to onlookers is that the onlooker remains aloof-he does not share their experience. Unless one does in imagination get inside the other man's mind, one will remain in ignorance.

Many satirical novels and plays come from an aloof (and therefore ignorant) observation of human nature. Briefly, the novelist in this instance does not understand the game. For example: suppose you are watching two respectable middle-aged men playing chess. You have never seen a game of chess. You know nothing about it. You don't know the difference between a bishop and a pawn. Well, you see one man push a tiny wooden figure, and the other man exhibit signs of acute dismay. Suddenly a look of rapturous triumph comes into his face, and he makes a move and the other man collapses. Of course you think both men are idiotic. Well, they are not; you do not understand the game.

You see and overhear two young lovers. Their conversation appears to be the last word in imbecility. That is because you are not in love. You laugh at them, but if you are in love yourself, you don't laugh; because love, whatever transport it may contain, has no humour. You watch a Salvation Army evangelist address a street crowd and become terribly excited. You look on from what you regard as a superior intellectual standpoint. But what this really means is that you haven't got his form of religion. In other words, you are ignorant. The realistic and satirical novelist describes an evangelist in bitter mockery, because the novelist has no religion, and therefore cannot share the other's fervour. But suppose this very evangelist could overhear the novelist discussing with some cronies in Greenwich Village "the art of the novel," and becoming terribly heated in the discussion, what would the evangelist think of such twaddle?

To a person who cares nothing about politics, a man in a state of political excitement appears silly. So one might go through the whole range of human passions, interests, and obsessions. What then is the answer? The answer is that if one really wishes to study human nature effectively, one must study it sympathetically. This is why Saint Paul said that

Charity was greater than Faith or Hope. By Charity he meant intellectual sympathy, the capacity to enter without prejudice into another's state of mind.

Finally, in spite of the selfish instincts of human nature, in spite of the bad record of every nation in the past and in the present, in spite of swindlers, liars, cowards, thieves, and murderers, it is with a thrill of admiration that we recall the names of certain individuals who have in their own lives and characters revealed the heroic possibilities of human nature; all men and women are potentially sublime, for every one has the divine spark.

FINIS

LONDON AS A SUMMER RESORT

I had an interesting conversation with Bernard Shaw last week. The next day he and Mrs. Shaw were leaving to spend the summer on the Riviera, which from time immemorial has been regarded as a winter resort. He gave, as is his custom, an original and diverting explanation of the fact that many now prefer to visit winter resorts in the summer. It is a matter of clothes. The Victorians were forced to go to cool places, or at any rate to avoid warm places; because they were compelled to wear stuffy clothes, the men being encased in frock coats, thick waistcoats, collars and swaddling neckcloths. But today, when one leaves off almost everything, the finest place in the world, according to G. B. S., is a climate where one can live outdoors in comfort, day and night. It is certainly true that many European resorts, where the hotels used to be open only during a short winter season, now attract visitors the year round. The converse is also true.

I can well remember when the great hotels of Switzerland-the playground of Europe-were open only during the summer; and were crowded only during the month of August. But now they never close and are as much sought after in December and January as in the good old summertime. The same is true of Lake Placid in America and of many other places. People in

Victorian times were forced to dress according to the prevailing style, which bore no reference to climate or common sense; remember how the women used to look, playing golf and term is!

Furthermore the old idea that everyone who could afford it must leave the city during the "heated term" has become obsolete, even in America. President Harper of the University of Chicago established a Summer Quarter, and professors who wished to do so could take their three months' vacation in the winter, a privilege that many continue to enjoy. The Country clubs and golf have had much to do with the contentment of business men who remain in cities during the summer. As a matter of fact, the city is not at all a bad place, I mean, of course, for those who can afford to snake themselves comfortable.

The city of Munich has for many years been a Mecca for summer pilgrims. The season of music, arranged for foreign visitors, reaches its climax in August. Now I wish to urge the millions of Americans who at one time or another cross the ocean to consider the merits of London as a summer resort.

For over a hundred years July has been a part of the London "season"; Parliament is in session, operas and theatres are open, and parties flourish amain. The twelfth of August, the opening of the grouse shooting season, is the formal beginning of the vacation; Parliament always adjourns for it, and London society flies north. But to an American London is day by day interesting, and there should be no closing of any season for him.

London has no prolonged hot weather, like St. Louis. It has been said that the English climate consists of eight months of winter, and four months of bad weather. This is an exaggeration. Every now and then there is a year when summer is omitted; but even in such an unfortunate time, one is better off in London than in the country. In fact, to an American London, while not the most beautiful city in the world, is assuredly the most interesting. It is inexhaustible. Every foot of it, to one well read in English literature, is hallowed ground; I think I could walk along Fleet street a thousand days in succession, and always receive a thrill.

I wish that every American journalist, every American book reviewer, every American drama critic, would spend a month in London and diligently read the morning newspapers, such as *The Times, The Telegraph, The Morning Post.* Every page seems to be written for intelligent readers. These London journalists review tennis, golf and cricket matches with more dignity than the average New Yorker reviews plays and books. One reason that militates steadily against intellectual progress in America is the fact that apparently we have no language suitable as a medium for the exchange of ideas. Our book reviews and our drama criticisms are too often written in a cheap kind of slang that is intended to be smart. If anyone imagines that the journalism of London loses in intensity by being written in suitable English, let him turn to a file of *The London Times* and read the story of Tilden playing tennis at Wimbledon.

A remarkable thing about literary society in London is that age has nothing to do with it. One meets in social gatherings men and women in the twenties and in the eighties-disparity in years seems to be forgotten.

One should remember that, owing to the small size of England, one can use London as a base of operations and take excursions into the country on the swift English trains, returning to London every evening; many happy, baggageless days have I spent in this manner.

When G. K. Chesterton was in America, I asked him what difference between the two countries impressed him most. Instantly he replied, "Your wooden houses." I had never thought of them as curiosities, but one does not see them in England. The thing that to me is most noticeable on the London streets is the absence of straw hats. There are many more bare male heads than there are straw hats. It is almost impossible to attract attention in London, but a straw hat will come nearest to doing the trick. Some men are exquisitely and others strangely clad, and nobody cares. I saw a man riding a bicycle. He had on tan shoes, homespun trousers, a frock coat, and a tall silk hat.

LOVE

NICODEMUS THE Scholar, a man of eminence and authority among the Jews, came to see Jesus by night. Why he chose the night no one knows; perhaps he wished to secure an uninterrupted interview, for during the day the Master was followed by importunate crowds. Possibly he feared some of his acquaintances might see him if he went by day, and he might therefore lose intellectual respect or social prestige. Perhaps he merely wanted a long and revealing talk, believing that the silent hours of the night beget intimacy. Little did the proud Pharisee imagine that when he acted on that impulse and called on the Teacher, he himself would be immortalised; yet such is the fact, for the words spoken on that memorable evening are heard and read today in the farthest corners of the earth.

What Nicodemus himself said is not so often quoted; yet he gave; a description of the Master that has perhaps never been surpassed; a description and a definition on which many Christians with divergent views today might unite. People differ very much as to what place in history should be given to Him, as to whence He came and who He was and as to His credentials.

But Nicodemus said, "We know that thou art a teacher come from God." How did Nicodemus know that? Well, how do we know in talking with a golf professional that he is a Scotsman? How do we know that a man is a Southerner? We know it by his accent, by his manner of speech, sometimes by the expression of his face or the cast of his features. The face and language of Jesus betrayed the country whence He came. The radiance of His countenance, the authoritative and yet tender tones of His voice, showed that the country of His origin was beyond the bounds of earthly geography. He brought into this world a divine atmosphere.

In the first act of the opera Lohengrin, when the solitary and apparently defenceless maiden Elsa is denounced by Telramund, she agrees, somewhat to the general consternation, to submit her cause to the ordeal of trial by combat. The trumpets sound, and there is silence. Who will be her champion? Again the trumpets sound. We hear the thrilling violins, and in the distance we see approaching a knight in silver armour. Elsa calls him the Divine Ambassador, der Gottgesandte; on his face and shining armour is the light that never was on sea or land.

Although Jesus was the ambassador from the kingdom of God to the kingdom of this world, and came to reveal to the children of men His Father's will, He never seemed interested in politics or in forms of government. No political party can claim Him. He was not a Conservative or a Radical, not a Republican or a Democrat or a Socialist. He came not to upset the structure of society, but to appeal to every individual human heart. He turned our sense of values upside down. Every valley shall be exalted, every hill shall be made low; the crooked shall be made straight, and the rough places plain. In this sense He was a revolutionist. He wished to establish a revolution in every individual mind; to change it from cowardice to courage, from slavery to independence, from vulgarity to beauty, from selfishness to unselfishness.

This Teacher who came from God was a specialist; He taught only one subject. The entire course of study contains only three words, but it takes a lifetime to learn it, and only a minority become experts. God is love. As I understand it, this is not intended to be a pretty or sentimental speech. It is not meant to be an optimistic motto, something to hang on the wall of an office, with the hope that it may kindle to renewed activity the flagging spirits of the observer. It is a philosophical principle, a core of thought. The Power whose influence is dimly discerned behind appearances, the Power that holds the stars in their places, the Power that controls the rise and ebb of the tides, the Power that keeps in accurate running order the mechanism of the universe, that Power is Love.

Hence one who loves God and his fellowmen is in connexion with the motive energy of the universe, with the Supreme Law.

What happens to a person when that idea enters and dominates his mind? Charles Dickens, who understood it better than most novelists, has given us plenty of illustrations, of which we may take one of the most familiar. On the day before Christmas, the financier Scrooge was, even for him, in a particularly unpleasant temper. One is apt to be like that, when one is out of sympathy with the prevailing mood of society. Scrooge in normal weather had the heart of a fish. He was not what we call responsive, demonstrative, expansive. He was acquisitive without being curious; he was not interested in what human beings were actually worth, but only in what they might be worth to him. When he entered a room men felt as one feels on the deck of a ship at night, in the proximity of an iceberg. Every one who met him was chilled and uncomfortable, and his departure brought a sense of relief.

Yet although every one who met him was ill at ease, he was more unhappy than they. They could escape him and his atmosphere; he could not run away from himself. In a dream that night true religion was revealed to him. He was born again. When he opened the window in the morning, the face of the world was changed. He thought it was a marvellous day. He saw a boy crossing the street and he thought him a marvellous boy. What a remarkable, what an unusual boy! His daily life became filled with zest and gusto; everything began to seem exciting, with a tang of adventure. For Scrooge there were no more dull days. Casual strangers on the street saluted him with a smile as of recognition, called forth by his radiant vitality. This is what happens when the love-lesson is learned and put into practice; it should always happen when one really "gets" religion. Scrooge had never imagined there could be such happiness merely in loving. For love is like an efficient furnace that warms every room of a large building.

The scientific evolutionists tell us that it has taken millions and millions of years to change an animal into a man. Love can do that in one second. When that predatory animal, Jean Valjean, stole the candlesticks in the night in the Bishop's House, and was caught next day by the police, they dragged him back to the Bishop's front door, with the evidences of his crime. The Bishop took a look at the wretched creature, and said to the policemen, "Why, I gave him those candlesticks." He lied like a gentleman, like a Christian.

The police are never shocked or puzzled by displays of vice and cruelty; their calloused eyes have looked on human nature at its worst. The only way to shock a policeman is to give him an exhibition of unexpected kindness or generosity. In this instance they were frankly amazed. But the Man of God insisted, and the officers of the law went away shaking their puzzled heads. Then the Bishop put his hand on the dull thief's shoulder and said, "Jean Valjean, my brother! you belong to God now." At that moment divine love entered his heart and changed him from an animal into a man. Love can do this, for it has transforming power. It can change a coward into a hero; it can change a despondent woman into a being full of zest, and it can do it in a moment.

Love is the only genuine test. Two hundred years ago many serious-minded people were agitated by this question-do I or do I not belong to the elect? Am I saved or am I damned? Well, the apostle John has given us in one of his letters a test at once simple and infallible; there can be no possible mistake. We know that we have passed from death unto life because we love the brethren. If we have love in the heart, sincere, unalloyed affection for others, free from hatred or jealousy, without a shade of resentment, then we know we are Christians. It is a searching test.

A widowed mother was living with her only son; they were the best of comrades, the most intimate of friends. But an adventuress got hold of the young man. She took away his money, his health, his position, his self-respect, and turned him into a vagabond. One day she told him that he must give her a supreme example of his devotion. He must murder his mother and bring to his mistress his mother's bleeding heart. Accordingly the young man went to his mother, killed her, cut the heart from her body, and holding it in his hand, hastened to the evil woman. In his haste he slipped on the pavement and fell headlong. The heart rolled out of his hand.

Then the heart spoke and said, "Did you hurt yourself, my dear son?"

If love is the supreme test of Christianity, then it is worse for a church member to show hatred than it is for him to indulge in the grosser vices. If a minister should enter the pulpit quite drunk, it would indeed be scandalous; it would be first-page news. But in reality it would be no worse than for him to show jealousy of other ministers, or to exhibit hatred toward some member of his church. If a deacon should attempt to pass the plate while drunk, it would be an abominable spectacle; but really it ought not to be more shocking than for him not to be "on speaking terms" with another member of the church, or to indulge in slanderous or spiteful or derogatory remarks. Such manifestations of evil are more contrary to the spirit of Christianity than drunkenness, and I have no mind to defend drunkenness.

If two members of the same church are living in hostility, that does not get into the newspapers, because, alas! it is not news. But it is ridiculously inconsistent with their profession. It simply won't do.

The letters of the apostle John show that he was a man of a beautiful and serene temper; but he was called a Son of Thunder. In his first epistle he used two terrible words-liar and murderer. And he was writing to church members.

"If a man say, I love God, and hateth his brother, he is a liar."

"Whosoever hateth his brother is a murderer."

It is idle to prate about loving God while we have malice in our hearts against our neighbors. It is indeed an absurdity, like a thief praying for success in his undertakings. But how does hatred make one a murderer?

It is really quite simple. Love is a creative force; it sees what is good, brings it out, encourages it, develops it. They say that Love is blind; but it is blind only to defects; it has in reality the sharpest and clearest vision, for it sees beauty where others see only ugliness it sees courage in obscure corners, and ;n commonplace minds it detects and recognizes the seeds of nobility. One cannot become a good critic of music unless one loves music; one will never understand men and women unless one begins by loving them. Perhaps one reason God understands men so perfectly is because He first loves them.

As all this is true of love, so it is true that hatred is desolating, crippling, destructive. Hatred blights everything it touches. It murders the souls of men and women, it destroys their good impulses, their awakening intelligence. If a teacher hates a pupil, he will destroy at birth every impulse to improvement in the pupil's mind, as an icy wind will destroy a tender plant.

In a recent English novel, This Day's Madness, a young girl comes running to her father in a state of excitement; "Oh, father, have you read Matthew Arnold's poem, The Forsaken Merman?" The father was reading the newspaper, and did not wish to be disturbed.

He said impatiently, "Yes, yes," and went on reading. "But, father-" she saw it was no use. That father was a murderer. He blew out the lamp of the girl's mind with the chill wind of indifference. Her soul was just being born, and he trampled on it; because he wanted to read a newspaper. If a little selfish indifference can kill like that, one can easily imagine the destructive power of hatred. We may be murderers.

There is nothing more valuable than the individual human soul. Hatred, resentment, or even indifference, may destroy it. On the other hand, love is not merely a creative force. It is the great preservative. Think of all the women (and men) who are trying vainly to look young; to reduce, to look agile, slender, active, graceful; and the harder they try the more depressing is the result. Yet if they had in their hearts real religion, the principle of love, they would have something eternally fresh. It is the only veritable fountain of youth that so many have sought in vain.

When the good housewives put up fruit in the summer, they do not preserve it with acids. They preserve it with sugar.

It takes something sweet to keep things fresh. What is a more unpleasant spectacle than the face of a sour old man or woman, where in addition to the ravages of time, there is the distortion of hate? And what is more beautiful than a face old in years, but alert in intelligence, eager in intellectual curiosity, and shining with benevolence?

"Nor Spring nor Summer's beauty hath such grace

As I have seen in one autumnal face."

The apostle John said "No man hath seen God at any time." We come nearest to seeing God when we see love, for where love is, there God is also. There is something inexpressibly sacred in an exhibition of sincere love, as if we were somehow in the presence of God. Two persons who love each other are in a place more holy than the interior of a church.

Tolstoi wrote a short story about a shoemaker, named Martin, who lived and worked in a basement. Out of his narrow window he could see only the boots and shoes of people who passed on the city pavement. Martin grew old. The members of his family were dead, and he was left alone. Like many lonely and forsaken individuals, he turned to the Gospels for relief and balm.

Every night, when the day's work was over, he would light his lamp, and read the words of divine comfort. His heart rose up within him; Jesus and the disciples became his companions. He used to think of the immense happiness of Peter and James and John because they actually saw their Lord day by day. "If I could only see the Master!" The next morning a poor fellow came into the shop, and it was clear that he was almost perishing with cold and hunger. Martin gave him tea and food and spoke encouraging words. The man went on his way with renewed hope and strength. Later there was the sound of a squabble on the street. Martin went out. A boy had stolen an apple from a poor old applewoman, and there was a fierce exchange of speech. She would have him arrested. Martin made the boy restore the apple, he induced the two antagonists to become friends, and they went away together laughing, the boy carrying the basket. Later he had another opportunity and took it.

That night, in accordance with his custom, Martin lit his lamp, and began to read the Gospels. Soon he was lost in thought. "If I could only see my Master!" Suddenly he felt that he was not alone in the room. He distinctly, heard a voice saying, "Why, Martin, Martin, don't you see Me? I have been with you all the day, long." Then Martin knew that his Saviour had visited him that day, and that he had received Him.

MAN AND BOY

F. P. A., in his excellent Conning Tower in the *New York World* for the Ides of March, pays a fine tribute to E. W. Howe and his paragraphs long ago in the Atchison *Globe.* He says: "There were two paragraphs that appeared just about the time we began reading the *Globe,* which we are willing to bet were written by Ed himself. He was less oracular in those days. They were something like the following:

'We have been editing a newspaper for twenty-five years, and have learned that the only thing a newspaper can safely attack is the man-eating shark.

A boy thinks, "What a fine time a man has!" And a man thinks, "What a fine time a boy has!" And what a rotten time they both have!' "

There is a strange reluctance on the part of most people to admit that they enjoy life. Having the honour of a personal acquaintance with both F. P. A. and Ed Howe, it is my belief they both had a happy childhood and that they are now having a good time in this strangest of all possible worlds. No one can judge another's inner state of mind, but as these distinguished humorists are men of unusually high intelligence I think they find life immensely interesting; and to be constantly interested is to be happy.

I remember a magnificent reply made by F. P. A. to a remark of that hirsute Englishman, D. H. Lawrence; the latter, commenting in that tactless fashion so characteristic of foreign visitors to these shores, said, "It must be terrible to be funny every day." "No," said F. P. A., "not so terrible as never to be funny at all."

I spent an agreeable afternoon in Florida talking with Ed Howe, or rather in hearing him talk. He told a succession of anecdotes and stories, and it was clear that he not only enjoyed telling them, which he did with consummate art, but that he enjoyed having them in his mind.

Why is it so many people are afraid to admit they are happy? I have a large and intimate acquaintance with farmers; many of them are splendid men. But how cautious they are in their replies to casual questions! If everything is going as well as could possibly be expected and you ask them how they are, they say, "Can't complain."

If a man says, "I have had and am having a happy life," he is regarded by many as being a shallow and superficial thinker; but if he says, "My most earnest wish is that I had never been born," many believe that he has a profound mind.

With regard to the saying quoted from the Atchison *Globe* that a boy thinks a man has a fine time and a man thinks a boy has a fine time and in reality both have a rotten time-well, the statement, whoever said it, is shallow and untrue. When I was a boy I had lots of fun, and I deeply pitied old men of thirty-two because I supposed they had no fun at all. Then, when I became a man, I realised how enormously richer in happiness is manhood than boyhood.

The average American boy has a pretty good time. What fun, on emerging from school on Friday afternoon, to know that tomorrow is Saturday! What fun to play games, to go on exploring adventures in neighbouring woods, to have picnics and jollifications, to live a life of active uselessness! The mere physical health of boyhood makes one feel like a young dog released from a chain. "Mere living" is good.

I remember seeing a picture of an old man addressing a small boy. "How old are you?" "Well, if you go by what Mama says, I'm five. But if you go by the fun I've had, I'm most a hundred."

Joseph Conrad, who was a grave and serious man, said he was neither an optimist nor a pessimist. He did not think life was perfect, but pessimism, he said, was intellectual arrogance. He made the point that no matter what was one's religion or philosophy, this at all events is a spectacular universe.

To deny life, to show no appreciation of it, seems to me both ungrateful and stupid. If you showed a man the Himalaya Mountains, the ocean in a storm, sunrise in the desert, the

Court of Honour in 1893, the Cathedral of Chartres, and he looked at them all with a lack-lustre eye, we should think him stupid. Well, the universe itself is tremendously spectacular, and the best shows in it are free. To go through life in rebellion, disgust or even in petulance, is the sign, not of a great, but of a dull mind.

How ridiculous it is for a boy to wish he were a man and how much more ridiculous for a man to wish he were a boy! It is as silly as crying for the moon. Instead of always longing for something beyond our reach, why not simply make the best of what we have? This would be a platitude if it were not that so very few people follow it.

There is certainly enough sorrow in the world, but I sometimes think we should enjoy life more if we had more of the divine gift of appreciation, if we were not so unappreciative. When Addison thanked God for the various pleasures of life, he thanked Him most of all for a cheerful heart.

More than two hundred years ago he wrote in the *Spectator:*

Ten thousand thousand precious gifts My daily thanks employ;

Nor is the least a cheerful heart That tastes these gifts with joy.

MARRIAGE

DURING FORTY YEARS Of teaching college undergraduates, if the lesson for the day was pertinent or an occasion afforded the opportunity, I annually gave one talk to the men in the classroom about their "careers," not concerning vocational training; what I emphasised was the right mental attitude toward life itself, the perhaps inarticulate philosophy underlying choices and ambitions.

I have always been able to speak more intimately to a group of young people than to an individual. The individual must take the initiative. I believe we have no more right to probe into the secret places of the heart than we have to pick a man's pocket. Whenever a student came to me alone and on his own, then I was willing and glad to discuss anything with him. But I believe every man's personality is sacred; an unauthorised or unasked-for attempt to enter it is the worst sort of trespassing.

In the classroom anything may be discussed without embarrassment. No teacher ever had a more intimate class room than mine. For my main interest in literature is its relation to men and women. Browning said his poetry dealt exclusively with the human soul; and it so happens that four poems of Tennyson, which, intentionally or not, are placed together, deal with four terrific passions. The poems are The First Quarrel, Rizpah, The Northern Cobbler, and The Revenge. They deal respectively with Sex, Mother-love, Drinking, and Patriotism. All four have produced happiness and all four have produced murder. Life is dangerous.

Students naturally wish to be successful in their chosen careers. I told them the greatest and most important career was Marriage. Unlike other careers, Marriage was a career open to every one of them. For among the many and striking differences between male and female, we may observe this: not every woman can be married but every man can. There is always some woman who will marry him.

The highest happiness on earth is in marriage. Every man who is happily married is a successful man even if he has failed in everything else. And every man whose marriage is a failure is not a successful man even if he has succeeded in everything else. The great Russian novelist, Turgenev, said he would give all his fame and all his genius if there were only one woman who cared whether he came home late to dinner. It would have been well if he had known this when he was young.

I told them, "Young gentlemen, although very few of you are now engaged to be married and not one of you is married, your wives are alive; they are living now. You do not know their names or where they are; but isn't it exciting to think that you are every moment drawing nearer to each other?

They are half an hour nearer you now than when you entered this classroom. Some in California are asleep for it is not yet dawn; some are eating breakfast in New York; some are eating lunch in Europe. But all your wives are as real as if you were already living with them. What do you intend to do about it?"

Those preparing for the law or medicine will take special studies; those preparing for athletic contests will take special training. If they did not, they would be idiotic. Those who are preparing for marriage should not leave success to chance. For while happiness is sometimes dependent on luck, in the majority of instances it is not. Happiness usually follows proper conditions.

Thus boys and girls, young men and women, will do well if, long before marriage, they train themselves mentally and physically to be successful husbands and wives. It is worth it; for they are in training for the highest prize obtainable on earth, and yet open to and won by millions.

However important sex instruction may be to those about to be married, there is one thing more important Character. Two people unselfish and considerate, tactful and warm-hearted, and salted with humour, who are in love, have the most essential of all qualifications for a successful marriage-they have Character. People who expect to be married need training in character more than they need instruction in sex.

From childhood boys and girls find out how children come, but the secret of a good character, temperament and disposition is not so readily discovered.

The reason Character is the most important requisite for success in marriage is not merely because it happens to be the chief support of happiness; but those who have character can turn an unsuccessful marriage into a successful

one, instead of taking the short way out, and acknowledging failure. No man or no woman is to blame for making a foolish marriage; it might happen to anyone. The test of character is not whether one has or has not made a foolish marriage, the test comes after a foolish marriage has been made. What a triumph then to turn that failure into a success, as the statesman turns a minority into a majority!

I am talking mainly to young people, for those who marry late in life either do not need suggestions or are already incurable. I am in favour of early marriages. I am delighted when either the boy's parents or those of the girl have money enough so that the young pair can be married at twentytwo, before they begin professional study or work. And when there is little money but either or both have a job, they should by all means be married. When young people marry, they take difficulties of housekeeping and privations as a lark, even as young people do camping out. When I was a boy, camping out was absolute bliss. Now it would be absolute horror. Furthermore, in youth neither of them has "set," they can accommodate themselves to each other.

The late President Harper of the University of Chicago was married at nineteen, not so young in his case, for he had already taken his doctor's degree. He told me that during the first five or six years, there were times when neither he nor his wife could write a letter, because they did not have enough cash to buy one postage stamp. He laughed aloud as he recounted this, and added, "There was never one moment when either of us regretted our marriage."

Marriage is a union between masculine strength and feminine loveliness. In the famous play The Barretts of Wimpole Street, Elizabeth exclaimed, "O Robert, how can you love me when you are so strong and I am so weak?" To which came the reply, "Elizabeth, my strength needs your weakness just as much as your weakness needs my strength." Spoken like the man he was. What is the value of being strong unless one can make good use of it? All good qualities grow by exercise.

It takes a great nature to love ardently and faithfully. Shakespeare's ideal soldier is Hotspur, the military hero of King Henry IV. Some of my readers may remember a play by Vicki Baum, called Grand Hotel. A weakling is informed by a physician that he has only a short time to live; whereupon he decides to "make the most of it" and plunges into dissipation. Everyone to his taste; but this is what Hotspur said:

> O gentlemen! the time of life is short,
>
> To spend that shortness basely were too long,
>
> If life did ride upon a dial's point,
>
> Still ending at the arrival of an hour.

Toward the close of the first scene of the third act, in the playful laughing dialogue between Hotspur and his wife, we see how happy and intimate was their home life; what perfect understanding existed between them. And he was one hundred per cent masculine.

One more illustration. The finest character in Homer's Iliad was not one of his own countrymen. It was the leader of the enemy. Hector, the Prince of Troy, was the ideal gentleman; if he were alive today, he would be the most popular undergraduate in any American or foreign university. It is said that morals change. They do not. I heard a Chinese scholar deliver an address on Mencius, who "flourished" in the fourth century before Christ. He set forth exactly the qualities that we like to think are characteristics of the best Americans. He upheld courage, modesty, unselfishness, consideration. There never was a time when by decent people these qualities were not considered superior to their opposites. Well, Hector was a shining example of their union in one man, and that man a great soldier, wholly masculine. Toward the close of Book VI of the Iliad Leaf's translation we see how beautiful was his home-life with his wife and little son. He came in the armour of battle to say farewell to both. "So she met him now, and with her went the handmaid bearing in her bosom the tender boy, the little child, Hector's loved son, like unto a beautiful star. . . . So now he smiled and gazed at his boy silently, and Andromache stood by his side weeping, and clasped her hand in his, and spake and called upon his name. Nay, Hector, thou art to me father and lady mother, yea and brother, even as thou art my goodly husband. Come now, have pity and abide here upon the tower, lest thou make thy child an orphan and thy wife a widow."

But Hector, telling her he loved her more than all, said he was the leader of the Trojan forces and must go out to fight. And he added something that makes everyone with sporting blood love him beyond words. He said he knew now that Troy could not win the war; they were all to be destroyed; but his duty was to fight just the same.

And then comes a scene of inexpressible tenderness. As he bent over to kiss the little boy, his son was terrified at the horse-hair plume on his father's helmet. "Then his dear father laughed aloud, and his lady mother." We hear that laughter across thirty centuries. Even in their anguish they laughed aloud, be cause the boy was for a moment afraid of his father. I wonder if a little son today was afraid of his father, would that seem to his parents so incredible?

"Forthwith glorious Hector took the helmet from his head, and laid it, all gleaming, upon the earth; then kissed he his dear son and dandled him in his arms." Then Hector said what every father for the last million years has said in his heart. He hoped the time would come when men would praise himself, Hector, but that they would say of his son, "Far greater is he than his father." Every normal father has longed to have his son become greater than he. Once a year I used to tell this Homeric story to my undergraduates and say, "Remember! you are carrying the family flag; at home there are those who hope that you will bring the greatest honour to the family name, far surpassing all who have gone before."

Marriage can be wonderful from every point of view, when it is a combination of the highest physical delight with the highest spiritual development. It is indeed the sublimation of the senses. The great novelist, George Meredith, who hated priggishness in all its forms, said in a letter, "I have written always with the perception that there is no life but of the spirit; that the concrete is really the shadowy; yet that the way to spiritual life lies in the complete unfolding of the creature, not in the nipping of his passions. An outrage to Nature helps to extinguish his light. To the flourishing of the spirit, then, through the healthy exercise of the senses."

Could there be a better description of the union of physical and spiritual development in marriage than his phrase The complete unfolding of the creature?

To his son Meredith wrote, "Look for the truth in everything, and follow it, and you will then be living justly before God. Let nothing flout your sense of a Supreme Being, and be certain that your understanding wavers whenever you chance to doubt that he leads to good. We grow to good as surely as the plant grows to the light.... Do not lose the habit of praying to the unseen Divinity. Prayer for worldly goods is worse than fruitless, but prayer for strength of soul is that passion of the soul which catches the gift it seeks."

What is love? Boys and girls fall in love at about the age of six or seven, and often while growing up, with a good many different persons. I say they fall in love for one does not have to explain to them what romantic love means. They have the symptoms described in the mediaeval romances, in novels, in love-poems, in sentimental songs.

But this is not exactly the same thing as married love which grows by companionship and by sharing sorrows as well as pleasures. Many years ago a college friend of mine, a splendid fellow with everything to make life worth living, was married to a fine girl. He died during the first weeks of the honeymoon. I said to a man of sixty, "Can anything be more tragic than that?" "Yes," he replied unhesitatingly, "it is more tragic when the husband or wife dies after twenty-five years of marriage."

He was accurate both ways; the loss after twenty-five years is more terrible; and in the instance I mentioned the shattered and desolated bride was in two years happily married to a second husband, which was right and wise.

The overwhelming passion of love is certainly rapture and marriage is its most satisfying consummation. But true love is not so expressive in desire for possession as it is in consideration for the welfare of the beloved object. "Oh, how I love you! " may not mean as much as "Don't go out without your rubbers on." Do you remember that passage in Guy de Maupassant where the husband said just that to his wife? And they were astounded when the maiden aunt who had lived with them for years without a word of dissatisfaction, who had gone in and out of the room as unremarked as the family cat, who was thought to be incapable of emotion, suddenly burst into a storm of weeping and cried, "No one has ever cared whether or not I had my rubbers on 1 "

Do you remember Browning's poem Muleykeh where the owner allowed his favourite mare, the Pearl, to be stolen when he could have overtaken her on an inferior horse, and his friends said he was a fool? He replied sobbing, "But she would have been beaten in speed You never have loved m y Pearl."

Is it love to dishonour a woman? Isn't it greed?

Yet expressions of love and passion, embraces and caresses, are also essential. I told my students, "After you are married, never leave the house, even if only to post a letter at the corner, without kissing your wife." This very simple act is an important preservative of married happiness.

I also advised them during the first twenty years of marriage to occupy the same bedroom. Quarrels and even insults given in the heat of anger are certain to happen in nine marriages out of ten. It is supremely important not to let these flames of resentment become a fatal conflagration. They must not last.

And blessings on the falling out,

Which all the more endears,

When we fall out with those we love,

And kiss again with tears!

Although happy marriages are common unhappy ones are still news), the only ideal, flawless marriages I ever heard of were those of the Brownings and the Hawthornes; in both instances the husbands were men of genius and the wives almost angelic.

Since the greatest of all the arts is the art of living together and since the highest and most permanent happiness depends on it, and since the way to practice this art successfully lies through character, the supreme question is how to obtain character.

The surest way is through Religion -Religion in the Home. All that we know for certain of every person is that he is imperfect. Human imperfection means a chronic need for improvement. The most tremendous and continuous elevating, purifying, strengthening force is Religious Faith.

My parents neglected my social training. I am sorry they did. They were careless about my clothes and my personal appearance. I am sorry for it. But I am constantly grateful for their religious and spiritual training. Every day of my life I am grateful. They knew it was more important than anything else in the world.

I was taken to church before I could walk; and as soon as I could walk I walked to church twice every Sunday, to church and Sunday School in the morning, to church again in the evening. My father asked a blessing on every meal, and conducted family prayers morning and evening. I began to read the Bible through when I was five years old. My father and mother read the Bible every day of their lives. I was brought up on Bible phrases; they were the stuff and substance of daily conversation.

I was baptized and joined the church when I was eleven; I have been a regular and active church-member ever since. I would rather belong to the church than belong to any other organisation or society or club. I would rather be a church-member than receive any honour or decoration in the world.

On a certain occasion, Ralph Waldo Emerson dropped in on a Sunday morning at a little country village church. It was only sparsely occupied, the people did not look brilliant, and the preacher was rather dull. At first he felt something akin to contempt for this apparently commonplace group. Suddenly it came over him that these people were assembled exclusively for the most important purpose that can inspire the human mind-the individual's personal relation to Almighty God. Then the little church and the little group took on an air of the sublime.

It amuses me when I read novels written by those who never had any religious faith or have lost it, novels that describe religious training in the home as producing unhappiness and hypocrisy and morbidity, with an atmosphere of thick gloom. As I look back on my childhood, it seems to me that the house was full of laughter. Table conversation was enlivened with mirth. If there ever was a merry household, it was ours. Our daily existence was full of fun, and Christmas, New Year's, Fourth of July, and birthdays were delirious.

This is normal and natural and logical. Religious faith is a central heating plant, it warms and energises one's whole existence. It gives a reason for life itself, for development. It gives a philosophy for conduct, and far more important, it emotionalises conduct, even more strongly than athletics and patriotism.

I am often called an optimist, and I suppose I am, because I believe that eventually Truth will conquer Error and Good conquer Evil. But I am not such an optimist as those who have no religious faith, who believe there is no future life, who believe there is no mind, no soul, no personality, only animal functions, and who yet are cheerful. I do not blame them for a loss of religious faith or of faith in survival, for everyone should believe what seems to him to be true; but to believe that human beings, whose minds are adapted for eternal development as the fish is adapted for water, yet have exactly the same fate as grasshoppers, and to remain cheerful under this assumption, requires an optimism that infinitely surpasses Pollyanna.

After listening once to a learned scientist delivering a lecture in which he used his brilliant mind to prove that he had no mind, I asked one who shared his belief, "I understand why you say all this; but why do you seem to enjoy it?"

"Ah," he replied, "we have such good times making our experiments." Exactly; exactly the way a child enjoys making mud pies, and with equal significance.

No, I rather admire the position taken by Edna St. Vincent Millay, who if I understand her correctly, has no religion. She wrote a poem about the death of those who are young and fair, and wrote with the defiance of despair. These things are so; but I will not be reconciled!

I admire the absolute pessimism of the great poet, A. E. Housman, who called himself an atheist, because he thought it was impossible that any god could be so utterly base as to create marvellous minds for a contemptible life and destiny.

Of all essential things, the most essential in married life and in the bringing up of children is Religion. When two people are engaged and are making plans for living together, they are sure to discuss religion. You remember how, suddenly Margaret turned to Faust and asked him point-blank, "Do you believe in God? Glaubst du an Gott?"

A chief reason why bringing up children is so difficult an art is that example is so much more important than precept. I am a qualified literary critic, although I never wrote a novel; I am a qualified drama critic, although I never wrote a play; I am a qualified baseball and lawn tennis critic, although I never was a first-class player. But when parents endeavour to bring up children to reflect honour on the family and to be useful members of society, the parents

must set a good example. Emerson said, "What you are thunders so loud I cannot hear what you say."

A man once wrote to Carlyle asking him if he ought to teach his little children to say their prayers. The austere Scot replied, "Yes, but only if you pray yourself. Don't teach them anything in which you yourself do not believe."

The Scot was right. To teach little children to say their prayers when the parents never say them themselves is like teaching a dog to say his prayers, a trick that seems to amuse many people. To have little children say grace at the table when no adult in the room has any faith is again only a pretty trick. But to send them to church when the parents stay away is far worse; it is culpable. Then the children regard church-going, praying, and religion as some of the innumerable burdens and penalties of childhood, from which they will escape as soon as they reach independence.

When Johnny Overton, the great Yale athlete, who was killed in the war, left his Tennessee home to go to college, his father told him that he would not give him any advice as to his morals or behaviour; "but, Johnny, will you promise me that you will never go to sleep at night until you have said your prayers?" John promised; and afterwards told his father he had kept his word.

If both young husband and wife share a similar religious belief, it is an enormous asset; an immense help to permanence in married happiness. Now one cannot believe in God and in Our Lord merely by wishing to do so. Yet I often think that many who do not believe do not really wish to with passionate earnestness; with as strong a wish as they have for money or for good looks or for popularity.

There are many who say and more who think without saying, "If I only had the faith I had as a child! Then I believed in God and in Jesus Christ and in heaven."

One might almost as well say, "if I only had the knowledge of algebra I had as a child!" Why do small boys and girls know algebra and why in later years do they not know it? Because when they were at school they gave their attention to it; they studied it; they thought about it. But thirty years have passed without their once opening the book or considering the subject.

I met a woman whom I had not seen since she was eighteen; and I asked her to play the piano. "Oh, I can't!" "But you used to play beautifully." "Yes, but I haven't touched the keys since I was married."

What does one expect? If one experiences regret for the lost faith of childhood, it is proper to ask, "How long is it since you read the Gospels? How long is it since you prayed?"

Since religious faith is such an asset to happiness, such a foundation for character and for married life and bringing up children, one might make an effort to recover it or at least to consider it.

I believe Sunday should be a day of joy and happiness; Sunday afternoon games and recreation are fine; but one enjoys them more if one has been to church in the morning or spent part of the day in either solitary or community worship. Those parents who selfishly seek only their own pleasures every week end, and who do nothing but amuse themselves, are they likely to bring up their children successfully?

To those who have no faith and to those who have lost it, let me recommend some wise words by Dean Inge.

There are those who are as explosively and suddenly "converted" as was St. Paul; but there are also those who cannot have such an experience; and many, many are the ways to God. One should give the matter serious attention; it deserves it. It is the most serious of all things.

Being educated means to prefer the best not only to the worst but to the second best. It means in music to prefer Beethoven not only to jazz but to Brahms. So it is in all forms of art, in athletics, in politics, in everything.

Now the Person celebrated in the Gospels is the greatest Personality in history. He knew more about life than Shakespeare. He was the greatest nerve specialist who ever lived. "Come unto me, . . . and you shall find rest unto your souls." His way is incomparably the best way; it is the way to peace of mind, to courage, independence, fearlessness, to joy. If we find faith lacking, try His way.

Listen to Dean Inge: he is discussing the illumination of the mind that follows recognition o f the Master. "Religious life begins with Faith, which has been defined ... as the resolution to stand or fall by the noblest hypothesis. This venture of the will and conscience progressively verifies itself as we progress on the upward path. That which began as an experiment ends as an experience. We become accustomed to breathe the atmosphere of the spiritual world."

If one follows the prescription of a physician and finds it beneficial, one believes in the physician.

Young people about to be married, young people recently married, young fathers and mothers should give Religion the most serious consideration. To neglect it, to be indifferent to it, is worse and more foolish than to be antagonistic. Religion is not a frill or an ornament or a luxury; still less is it a thing to clutch at only in danger or in heartbreak.

Religion is the greatest creative force in the world; it has made thousands of saints and thousands of heroes; it has revolutionised innumerable individual lives. It has changed people from selfishness to unselfishness; from cowardice to courage; from despair to hope; from vulgarity to decency; from barrenness of life to fruitfulness.

Religious faith has produced the finest architecture, the finest painting, the finest music, the finest literature in the world. When Religion can change the lives of millions, when it can produce supreme creations in art, it is a force worth serious consideration.

The late John Philip Sousa, the famous composer and bandmaster, said that the reason why there was not so much great music produced in the twentieth as in the nineteenth century, was because religious faith had declined. According to him, creation is based on faith. This may be claiming too much, but his testimony as a composer is interesting.

Religion is not a dream or an illusion or a phantasy. I saw a quotation from Doctor Jung's book, Psychology and Religion, which runs as follows: "Religious experience is absolute and indisputable and must signify something related to the archetype or unconscious mental background of all of us." In this sentence the word archetype means an objective Reality, like a Model of which individual examples are imitations.

The American philosopher, Paul Elmet More, who died in 1937, and who was one of the most profound scholars in the world, after prolonged thought and study and observation, came from agnosticism into a complete and passionate faith in the Christian religion and in the Incarnation. He said that while Love was the main principle in religion as a way of life, the most important contribution to humanity made by religion was Hope. Hope in the destiny of man, in the superlative value of the individual, in the personality of our Father in Heaven.

I might add that if hope deferred maketh the heart sick, hope destroyed maketh the heart dead.

The very last word to describe religious faith is the word anesthetic. Religious faith is a comfort to the old, the sick, and the suffering; but in general it is not a sedative, it is a tonic. It is a dynamo; it is a driving force. Henry Drummond, the most effective speaker on religion I can remember, said to a group of students, "I ask you to become Christians not because you may die tonight, but because you are going to live tomorrow. I come not to save your souls, but to save your lives."

Lord Charnwood, the famous biographer of Lincoln, a scholar and a business man, said he took up the Gospel of St. John, and as a professional writer of biography, studied it impartially. The result was, "I found myself at the end

just an ordinary Christian." And he wrote a book called According to St. John.

Religion adds an enormous zest to daily life; it makes everything interesting and significant. It keeps alive the capacity of wonder. I myself am interested in everything in the world, from a sandlot ball game to the nebula in Orion. But the mainspring of my existence, the foundation of my happy and exciting life, is Christian faith.

I suggest to those recently married and those about to be married that they are entering into a relationship that can bring them the highest and most lasting happiness or the most crushing disillusion and despair. Such a relationship is particularly remarkable because of its intimacy, an intimacy far transcending that of friendship, love of parents or any earthly emotion. As Thomas Hardy said, Marriage annihilates reserve. In this amazing intimacy, every care should be taken to ensure success. A common interest in religion, saying prayers together, will help enormously toward increasing and preserving happiness.

For a true belief in the Christian religion will improve daily manners. Husband and wife will not take each other for granted; they will not become stodgy or commonplace or stereotyped. The man will not use the newspaper at the breakfast table as a screen. Bad table manners have caused many divorces.

Tennyson has given us in The Princess the real kind of marriage which one of my students described in the vernacular. He wrote to me, "I am going to be married. It won't be much of a wedding, but it will be a wonderful marriage."

Listen to Tennyson:

For woman is not undevelopt man,

But diverse: could we make her as the man,

Sweet Love were slain: his dearest bond is this,

Not like to like, but like in difference.

Yet in the long years liker must they grow;

The man be more of woman, she of man:

He gain in sweetness and in moral height,

Nor lose the wrestling thews that throw the world;

She mental breadth, nor fail in childward care,

Nor lose the childlike in the larger mind;

Till at the last she set herself to man,

Like perfect music unto noble words.

A wife may be a civilising force; that is well; but she may be far more than that. She may be a revelation in daily intimacy more unconsciously impressive than a professional saint.

This is what Caponsacchi said of an imagined union with Pompilia:

To live, and see her learn, and learn by her,

Out of the low obscure and petty world

Or only see one purpose and one will Evolve themselves i' the world, change wrong to right;

To have to do with nothing but the true,

The good, the eternal-and these,

not alone In the main current of the general life,

But small experiences of every day,

Concerns of the particular hearth and home:

To learn not only by a comet's rush

But a rose's birth, -not by the grandeur,

God, But the comfort, Christ.

THE END

MOLASSES

Before both the word molasses and the thing it signifies disappear forever from the earth, I wish to recall its flavour and its importance to the men and women of my generation. By any other name it would taste as sweet; it is by no means yet extinct; but for many years maple syrup and other commodities have taken its place on the breakfast table. Yet I was brought up on molasses. Do you remember, in that marvellous book, *Helen's Babies,* when Toddie was asked what he had in his pantspocket, his devastating reply to that tragic question? He calmly answered, "Bread and molasses."

Well, I was brought up on bread and molasses. Very often that was all we had for supper. I well remember, in the sticky days of childhood, being invited out to supper by my neighbour Arthur Greene. My table manners were primitive and my shyness in formal company overwhelming.

When I was ushered into the Greene dining room not only as the guest of honour but as the only guest, I felt like Fra Lippo Lippi in the most august presence in the universe, only I lacked his impudence to help me out.

The conditions of life in those days may be estimated from the fact that the entire formal supper, even with "company," consisted wholly and only of bread, butter and molasses. Around the festive board sat Mr. Greene, a terrifying adult who looked as if he had never been young; Mrs. Greene, tight-lipped and serious; Arthur Greene, his sister Alice, and his younger brother, Freddy. As I was company I was helped first and given a fairly liberal supply of bread, which I unthinkingly (as though I were used to such luxuries) spread with butter and then covered with a thick layer of molasses. Ah, I was about to learn something.

Mr. Greene turned to his eldest son, and enquired grimly, "Arthur, which will you have, bread and butter or bread and molasses?"

The wretched Arthur, looking at my plate, and believing that his father, in deference to the "company," would not quite dare to enforce what was evidently the regular evening choice, said, with what I recognised as a pitiful attempt at careless assurance, "I'll take both."

"No, you don't!" countered his father, with a tone as final as that of a judge in court. His father was not to be bluffed by the presence of company; he evidently regarded discipline as more important than manners. The result was I felt like a voluptuary, being the only person at the table who had the luxury of both butter and molasses. They stuck in my throat; I feel them choking me still, after an interval of more than fifty years.

The jug of molasses was on our table at home at every breakfast and at every supper. The only variety lay in the fact (do you remember?) that there were two distinct kinds of molasses-sometimes we had one, sometimes the other.

There was Porto Rico molasses and there was New Orleans molasses-brunette and blonde.

The Porto Rico molasses was so dark it was almost black, and New Orleans molasses was golden brown.

The worst meal of the three was invariably supper, and I imagine this was fairly common among our neighbours. Breakfast was a hearty repast, starting usually with oatmeal, immediately followed by beefsteak and potatoes or mutton chops, sometimes ham and eggs; but usually beef or chops. It had a glorious coda with griddle cakes or waffles; and thus stuffed, we rose from the table like condors from their prey, and began the day's work. Dinner at one was a hearty meal, with soup, roast, vegetables and pie.

Supper consisted of "remainders." There was no relish in it, and I remember that very often my mother, who never complained vocally, looking at the unattractive spread with lack-lustre eye, would either speak to our one servant or would disappear for a moment and return with a cold potato, which it was clear she distinctly preferred to the sickening sweetish "preserves" and cookies or to the bread and molasses which I myself ate copiously.

However remiss and indifferent and selfish I may have been in my conduct toward my mother-and what man does not suffer as he thinks of this particular feature of the irrecoverable past? -it does me good to remember that, after I came to man's estate, I gave my mother what it is clear she always and in vain longed for in earlier years, a good substantial dinner at night.

At breakfast we never put cream and sugar on our porridge; we always put molasses. Then, if griddle cakes followed the meat, we once more had recourse to molasses. And as bread and molasses was the backbone of the evening meal, you will see what I mean when I say I swam to manhood through this viscous sea. In those days youth was sweet.

The transfer of emphasis from breakfast to supper is the chief distinguishing change in the procession of meals as it was and as it became.

It now seems incredible that I once ate large slabs of steak or big chops at breakfast, but I certainly did. And supper, which approached the vanishing point, turned into dinner in later years.

Many, many years ago we banished the molasses jug and even the lighter and more patrician maple syrup ceased to flow at the breakfast table. I am quite aware that innumerable persons still eat griddle cakes or waffles and syrup at the first meal of the day. It is supposed that the poet-artist Dante Gabriel

Rossetti ruined his health by eating huge portions of ham and eggs, followed by griddle cakes and molasses, for breakfast. To me there has always been something incongruous between syrup and coffee; they are mutually destructive; one spoils the taste of the other.

Yet waffles and syrup are a delectable dish; and I am quite certain that nectar and ambrosia made no better meal. What to do, then? The answer is simple. Eat no griddle cakes, no waffles and no syrup at breakfast; but use these commodities for dessert at lunch. Then comes the full flavour.

Many taverns now have hit upon the excellent idea of serving only two dishes for lunch or dinner-chicken and waffles. This obviates the expense of waste, the worry of choice, the time lost in plans. And what combination could possibly be better?

One of the happiest recollections of my childhood is the marvelous hot, crisp waffle lying on my plate, and my increasing delight as I watched the molasses filling each square cavity in turn.

As the English poet remarked, "I hate people who are not serious about their meals."

WILLIAM LYON PHELPS SPEAKS ON BOOKS

FROM A RADIO BROADCAST ON APRIL 6, 1933

The habit of reading is one of the greatest resources of mankind; and we enjoy reading books that belong to us much more than if they are borrowed. A borrowed book is like a guest in the house; it must be treated with punctiliousness, with a certain considerate formality. You must see that it sustains no damage; it must not suffer while under your roof. You cannot leave it carelessly, you cannot mark it, you cannot turn down the pages, you cannot use it familiarly. And then, some day, although this is seldom done, you really ought to return it.

But your own books belong to you; you treat them with that affectionate intimacy that annihilates formality. Books are for use, not for show; you should own no book that you are afraid to mark up, or afraid to place on the table, wide open and face down. A good reason for marking favorite passages in books is that this practice enables you to remember more easily the significant sayings, to refer to them quickly, and then in later years, it is like visiting a forest where you once blazed a trail. You have the pleasure of going over the old ground, and recalling both the intellectual scenery and your own earlier self.

Everyone should begin collecting a private library in youth; the instinct of private property, which is fundamental in human beings, can here be cultivated with every advantage and no evils. One should have one's own bookshelves, which should not have doors, glass windows, or keys; they should be free and accessible to the hand as well as to the eye. The best of mural decorations is books; they are more varied in color and appearance than any wallpaper, they are more attractive in design, and they have the prime advantage of being separate personalities, so that if you sit alone in the room in the firelight, you are surrounded with intimate friends. The knowledge that they are there in plain view is both stimulating and refreshing. You do not have to read them all. Most of my indoor life is spent in a room containing six thousand books; and I have a stock answer to the invariable question that comes from strangers. "Have you read all of these books?" *"Some of them twice."* This reply is both true and unexpected.

There are of course no friends like living, breathing, corporeal men and women; my devotion to reading has never made me a recluse. How could it? Books are of the people, by the people, for the people. Literature is the immortal part of history; it is the best and most enduring part of personality. But book-friends have this advantage over living friends; you can enjoy the most truly aristocratic society in the world whenever you want it. The great dead are beyond our physical reach, and the great living are usually almost as inaccessible; as for our personal friends and acquaintances, we cannot always see them. Perchance they are asleep, or away on a journey.

But in a private library, you can at any moment converse with Socrates or Shakespeare or Carlyle or Dumas or Dickens or Shaw or Barrie or Galsworthy. And there is no doubt that in these books you see these men at their best. They wrote for you. They "laid themselves out," they did their ultimate best to entertain you, to make a favorable impression. You are necessary to them as an audience is to an actor; only instead of seeing them masked, you look into their innermost heart of heart."

William Lyon Phelps - 1933

ONE DAY AT A TIME

On a certain morning in the year 1900 I called on President Eliot at his office in Harvard University.

He was in a gracious mood and we talked of many things. As I rose to leave I said I hoped I might always have the privilege of calling on him whenever I came to Cambridge.

He remarked gravely (in every sense of that word): "The next time you come I may not be here."

"What's the matter? Are you going to re-sign?" "Resign? Certainly not. But, remem-ber, I am sixty-six years old." The only answer to that was a laugh, which I provided spontaneously.

Now if the distinguished president of Harvard had known then that twenty-five years after this interview, he would be in the full possession of his physical and mental faculties, even though he had ceased to possess the Harvard one, he would have wasted not a single moment on the thought of his approaching death. And if gold rusts, what shall iron do?

In the eighteenth century, the poet Young was an intimate friend of the novelist Richardson and their correspondence has a certain mortuary interest. For Young's letters are as gloomy as his verses; they are largely taken up with predicting his own speedy death, which, however, Richardson awaited in vain, as the aged poet survived him. In his own last moments Richardson may have felt something akin to resentment at having wasted his sympathy on one who would attend his funeral.

We look backward too much and we look for-ward too much. Thus we miss the passing mo-ment.

In our regrets and apprehensions, we miss the only eternity of which man can be absolutely sure, the eternal Present. For it is always NOW. As Browning's clever Bishop Blougram remarked

> Do you know, I have often had a dream
>
> (work it up in your next month's article)
>
> Of man's poor spirit in its progress, still
>
> Losing true life forever and a day
>
> Through ever trying to be and ever being-In
>
> the evolution of successive spheres-Before

its actual sphere and place of life,

Halfway into the next, which having reached

It shoots with corresponding foolery

Halfway into the next still, on and off!

As when a traveller, bound from North to South,

Scouts fur in Russia; what's its use in France?

If France spurns flannel; what's its need in Spain?

If Spain drops cloth, too cumbrous for Algiers!

Linen goes next, and last the skin itself,

A superfluity in Timbuctoo.

When, through his journey, was the fool at ease?

When Thoreau was questioned as to his beliefs in a life beyond the grave, he answered impatiently, "Oh, one world at a time." I was deeply impressed in reading Dr. Cushing's admirable biography of Sir William Osler, to see that the physician and philosopher laid the greatest stress on living one day at a time.

That was his summary of the art of living, for all those who wished to accomplish as much as possible, and retain their peace of mind: Live one day at a time.

I remember, when I was twenty years old, I wasted many good hours in speculating on what I should do after graduation from college, which event was two years ahead. An old man told me not to give it a moment's thought: "You can-not decide what to do till the emergency comes."

Meanwhile there was the daily work. The best way to prepare for the future was to do that well, rather than waste one's energies on idle worry. "Give us this clay our daily bread." There are always gloomy prophets who can-not enjoy the present moment, because they are so sure trouble is coming. The winter of 1917-1918 was the coldest in my recollection; and many said, "Well, the climate is changing and we must not expect any mild winters." Then came the winter of 1918-1919, which was the mildest in my recollection. And how distinctly I recall conversations like the following. Along about Christmastide, I would say, "What a beautiful winter!" and in every instance, without a single exception, I got the reply, "Just wait. We'll catch it later." Then when the weather continued sweet all through January, I made the same remark to different individuals, and always got a warning for my pains. But the evil came not at all. My friends had determined to be miserable. They could not enjoy a lovely mild season, for in its loveliness they shook with the chill of apprehension.

The fear of life is the favourite disease of the twentieth century. Too many people are afraid of tomorrow-their happiness is poisoned by a phantom. Many are afraid of old age, forgetting that even if they should lose their bodily vigour, weakness itself may minister to the development of the mind and spirit. In the words of the aged poet Waller,

The soul's dark cottage, battered and decayed,

Lets in new light through chinks that time has made.

Stronger by weakness, wiser men become,

As they draw near to their eternal home.

Let the scientists worry about our origin-slime, monkeys, what not; let the prophets worry about our future-"the decline of western civilisations," and what not. Some people are alarmed because in nine thousand billion years the sun's fuel may give out. Instead of chagrin over our past, and alarm over our future, suppose we consider our opportunity.

Listen to Emerson: "Write it on your heart that every day is the best day in the year. No man has earned anything rightly until he knows that every day is doomsday. Today is a king in disguise. Today always looks mean to the thoughtless, in the face of a uniform experience that all good and great and happy actions are made up precisely of these blank todays. Let us not be deceived, let us unmask the king as he passes."

Our Lord, in his daily conversations, was al-ways drawing the attention of his listeners away from vague speculations, to the present moment and the present opportunity. To such absurd enquiries as, "Whose wife shall she be in heaven?" he said, "God is not the God of the dead, but of the living." To the man who said that he must postpone action until he had attended a funeral, the Master replied crisply, "Let the dead bury the dead and come and follow me." And after an enumeration of the various worries about the future with which men and women torment their minds, he said, "Take no

thought for the morrow." Do not worry about the future. He added, significantly, that if we are determined to look for trouble, we can find it today without waiting for tomorrow.

PROFESSION AND PRACTICE

Beautiful lines which show that the man who wrote them had a clear conception of true religion are these

Thus to relieve the wretched was his pride,

And even his failings leaned to virtue's side;

But in his duty prompt at every call,

He watched and wept,

he prayed and felt for all;

And, as a bird each foud endearment tries

To tempt its new-fledged offspring to the skies,

He tried each art,

reproved each dull delay,

Allured to brighter worlds, and led the way.

The man who wrote them is thus described by James Boswell: "Those who were in any way distinguished excited envy in him to so ridiculous an excess that the instances of it are hardly credible. When accompanying two beautiful young ladies with their mother on a tour of France, he was seriously angry that more attention was paid to them than to him." Goldsmith wrote of virtue, modesty, sweet unselfishness in the most convincing manner; his words were more convincing than his behaviour. He allured to brighter worlds, but did not lead the way.

Schopenhauer, the great philosopher of pessimism, taught that absolute asceticism was the only true religion and method of escape from the ills of life; but he never practiced it, and told his disciples to mind his precepts and not his example. Unfortunately, whenever any one gives advice in the field of morality or religion, the first person on whom we test its practical value is the preacher. Emerson remarked, "What you are thunders so loud I cannot hear what you say."

No great writer of modern times has written more persuasively of the Christian way of life than Tolstoi; there is no doubt that his stories and tracts have had an immense influence on millions of readers and have inspired them toward unselfishness, kindness and humility. But of all great Russian writers, Tolstoi himself was the most difficult to get along with; he could not bear to hear any other writer praised and was lacking in the grace of appreciation. His rival, Turgenev, who had no religious belief of any kind, excelled Tolstoi in the virtues of modesty, unselfishness and consideration for others.

One of the many reasons why the art of bringing up children is the most difficult of all arts is that it is essential for parents to set a daily example. All the moral precepts in the world will not seriously impress children if their parents do not in their daily life come somewhere near the ideals they hold up. The child will after a fashion love his parents anyhow, but as he grows older and begins to compare what he has been taught with what he sees, the child is transformed into a judge. This partly explains that fear of their own children which so many parents secretly feel.

If the parents make their small children go to church and stay home themselves, the children quite naturally regard church-going as one of the numerous penalties imposed on youth and look forward to maturity as an escape from this and many other unpleasant compulsions. If parents impress on their children the necessity of telling the truth, they must not themselves tell lies; they are being watched by the sharpest eyes in the world.

Although in a certain sense we are all hypocrites-for no one can live up to his ideals-we hate any flagrant case of hypocrisy. I suppose one reason we have a sneaking admiration for pirates is that pirates are not hypocrites. There is no doubt that professional pirates are more generally admired than professional politicians.

I do not say that politicians are hypocrites; I say that pirates are not.

It is the personalities of great leaders, much more than their sayings, that have had a beneficial influence. The sayings of Jesus very word that has come down to us-can be read through in three hours. But from His life and character flows a vital force, tremendously effective after nineteen centuries. Very few people read the literary compositions of Sir Philip Sidney, but millions have been influenced by his life and character. The pure, unselfish life of George Herbert is more efficacious than his poems; and consider Saint Francis!

The Christian Church has had in every century of its existence able, honest, determined foes, who have done their best to destroy it; it is probable that they have done it no injury. Nor have the frank sensualists and materialists hurt it at all. It has been injured only by its professed friends.

If a physician opens an office, his most dangerous foes are not his competitors, that is to say, other doctors; his most dangerous foes are those of his patients who say, "Well, I took his medicine, and it did me no good." The best advertising is done by one's sincere friends and admirers; the good word about the new doctor, or the new novel, or the new play, is passed along.

The Christian religion professes to make those who accept it better and happier; every one who professes it and exhibits none of its graces is a powerful argument against its validity. A man's foes are those of his own household.

Sometimes I think religion should first of all show itself in good manners; that is, in true politeness, consideration for others, kindness and deference without servility. Such persons are those we love to meet and be with; they are good advertisements of their religion; they will not have to talk about it because its effects are so plainly and attractively seen.

SPIRITUAL HEALING

I believe that the average man or woman today needs one thing more than he needs anything else-spiritual healing. I believe this is truer of the men and women of our age than of those of any preceding epoch-and I believe they need it more than they need material luxuries, increase of mechanical resources, yes, more than they need mental tonics or emotional inspiration.

The people of the United States are suffering from "nerves." Now the casualties in diseases of the nerves are large, because, as is well known, in cases of nervous prostration everybody dies except the patient. I shall not say that America won the war, but anyhow America was on the winning side. We were triumphantly victorious; we are the only rich and prosperous nation on earth. Americans are the only people in the world who are physically comfortable in bad weather. But although there is a steady increase in physical luxuries, I am not sure of a steady increase in serene happiness, in the calm that comes from mental contentment, in an approach toward universal peace of mind. What shall we say of a prosperous and rich nation whose prosperity and wealth are accompanied by an epidemic of suicide?

We are overwrought, tense, excited; our casual conversations are pimpled with adjectives; our letters are written in italics, and-a sure sign of fever-there has been an increase in cursing and swearing. Many respectable persons show a proficiency in this verbal art that used to be chiefly characteristic of lumberjacks and longshoremen. We become colossally excited about trivial things.

Sometimes when I find myself in a state of almost insane irritation over some trifle I seem to hear the quiet voice of Emerson speaking from the grave-Why so hot, little man?

In a charming comedy by Clare Kummer, in which that beautiful and accomplished actress the late Lola Fisher took the leading part, one of her speeches explained that when she was a child her mother told her that whenever she felt herself rising to a boiling point she must stop for a moment and say aloud, "Be calm, Camilla." That was the name of the play, "Be Calm, Camilla"-and there are many Camillas who need that relaxation.

It is characteristic of the American temperament that it needs mental sedatives more than spurs; and yet thousands of Americans are looking around all the time for something with a "kick" in it. How often we hear in casual conversation the phrase, "I got a fearful kick out of that." What they need is not a kick, but a poultice; not a prod, but a cool, healing hand. Although Americans need healing more than the men and women of any other nation, there are times when ahnost any person would profit by such treatment. The experience of John Stuart Mill is not unusual. He was carefully brought, up by his father without religious training. When he was twenty-five years old he fell into a state of profound depression. A cloud of melancholia settled on his mind and heart, so that he not only lost interest in life but felt that the world had no meaning. We know that King Saul was relieved from the evil spirit of nervous melancholy by music; but Mill loved music, and yet in his crisis music failed him.

Fortunately, he turned to the poetry of Wordsworth. Now of all the great poets Wordsworth is the best healer, because he drew balm from objects within everybody's reach. The "Nature" that Wordsworth writes about does not require a long and expensive journey, like going South in winter or travelling to distant mountains. This poet wrote about the simple things in nature-the things that can be seen from the front door or from the back yard.

The novelist George Gissing, who had been chronically tortured by two desperate evils, grinding poverty and ill health, was, owing to a fortunate circumstance, able to live in solitude for a time in the charming county of Devon, in southwest England. The result of his meditations appeared in a book, first published in 1903, called *The Private Papers o f*

Henry Ryecroft. This is a book of healing, and I recommend it to everybody, for I do not know any one who could not profit by it. As Mill had suffered from intellectual depression and been cured by Wordsworth, so Gissing, who had suffered from poverty and sickness, cured himself by preserving the fruit of his communion with nature:

I had stepped into a new life. Between the man I had been and that which I now became there was a very notable difference. In a single day I had matured astonishingly; which means, no doubt, that I suddenly entered into conscious enjoyment of powers and sensibilities which had been developing unknown to me.

"I had matured astonishingly." Isn't that what is really the matter with us, that we haven't grown up? We are like children crying for the moon, when the riches of the earth are within our reach. Our pursuit of excitement and our resultant sufferings are largely childish. It is unfortunate to suffer from infantile diseases when we are old.

I have been reading a new novel, a book of healing, which most new novels are not. It is curious that so many are eagerly reading new novels and seeing new plays whose only purpose is to stimulate animal instincts which need no stimulation. Or they are reading new novels which distress and torment a mind already tumultuously confused. Be calm, Camilla.

The book I allude to was published in 1927. It is called *Winterwise* and is written by Zephine Humphrey. It describes a winter spent in a lonely farmhouse in Vermont, a State not yet famous as a winter resort-except for those who think only of winter in connexion with violent athletics. The book is full of deep, tranquil wisdom. It points out sources of abiding happiness-happiness that no disaster can permanently remove.

SUNRISE

At an uncertain hour before dawn in February 1912, as I lay asleep in my room on the top floor of a hotel in the town of Mentone, in Southern France, I was suddenly awakened by the morning star. It was shining with inquisitive splendour directly into my left eye. At that quiet moment, in the last stages of the dying night, this star seemed enormous. It hung out of the velvet sky so far that I thought it was going to fall, and I went out on the balcony of my room to see it drop. The air was windless and mild, and, instead of going back to bed, I decided to stay on the balcony and watch the unfolding drama of the dawn. For every clear dawn in this spectacular universe is a magnificent drama, rising to a superb climax.

The morning stars sang together and I heard the sons of God shouting for joy. The chief morning star, the one that had roused me from slumber, recited a splendid prologue. Then, as the night paled and the lesser stars withdrew, some of the minor characters in the play began to appear and take their respective parts. The grey background turned red, then gold. Long shafts of preliminary light shot up from the eastern horizon, and then, when the stage was all set, and the minor characters had completed their assigned roles, the curtains suddenly parted and the sun-the Daystar-the star of the play, entered with all the panoply of majesty. And as I stood there and beheld this incomparable spectacle, and gazed over the mountains, the meadows and the sea, the words of Shakespeare came into my mind

> Full many a glorious morning have I seen,
> Flatter the mountain tops with sovereign eye.
> Kissing with golden face the meadows green.
> Gilding pale streams with heavenly alchemy.

It is a pity that more people do not see the sunrise. Many do not get up early enough, many do not stay up late enough. Out of the millions and millions of men, women and children on this globe only a comparatively few see the sunrise, and I dare say there are many respectable persons who have never seen it at all. One really should not go through life without seeing the sun rise at least once, because, even if one is fortunate enough to be received at last into heaven, there is one sight wherein this vale of tears surpasses the eternal home of the saints. "There is no night there," hence there can be no dawn, no sunrise; it is therefore better to make the most of it while we can.

As a man feels refreshed after a night's sleep and his morning bath, so the sun seems to rise out of the water like a giant renewed. Milton gave us an excellent description:

So sinks the daystar in the ocean bed, And yet anon repairs his drooping head,

And tricks his beams, and with new-spangled ore Flames in the forehead of the morning sky.

Browning, in his poem, Pippa Passes, compares the sunrise to a glass of champagne, a sparkling wine overflowing the world:

DAY!

Faster and more fast,

O'er night's brim,

day boils at last:

Boils, pure gold,

o'er the cloud-cup's brim,

Where spurting and suppressed it lay,

For not a froth-flake touched the rim

Of yonder gap in the solid gray

Of the eastern cloud, an hour away;

But forth one wavelet,

then another, curled.

Till the whole sunrise,

not to be suppressed,

Rose, reddened, and its seething breast Flickered in bounds, grew gold, then overflowed the world.

The sunset has a tranquil beauty but to me there is in it always a tinge of sadness, of the sadness of farewell, of the approach of darkness. This mood is expressed in the old hymn which in my childhood I used to hear so often in church Fading, still fading, the last beam is shining, Father in heaven! the day is declining. Safety and innocence fly with the light, Temptation and danger walk forth with the night.

Sorrow may endure for a night, but joy cometh in the morning, saith the Holy Book. The sunrise has not only inexpressible majesty and splendour, but it has the rapture of promise, the excitement of beginning again. Yesterday has gone forever, the night is over and we may start anew. To how many eyes. weary with wakefulness in the long watches of the night, or flushed with fever, is the first glimmer of the dawn welcome. The night makes every fear and worry worse than the reality, it magnifies every trivial distress. Mark Twain said the night brought madness-none of us is quite sane in the darkness. That particular regret for yesterday or apprehension for tomorrow that strikes you like a whiplash in the face at 2:45 A.M. dwindles into an absurdity in the healthy dawn.

Mark Twain, who had expressed the difference between the night and the morning tragically, also expressed it humorously. He said that when he was lying awake in the middle of the night he felt like an awful sinner, he hated himself with a horrible depression and made innumerable good resolutions; but when at 7:30 he was shaving himself he felt just as cheerful, healthy and unregenerate as ever.

I am a child of the morning. I love the dawn and the sunrise. When I was a child I saw the sunrise from the top of Whiteface and it seemed to me that I not only saw beauty but heard celestial music. Ever since reading in George Moore's Evelyn Innes the nun's description of her feelings while listening to Wagner's Prologue to *Lohengrin* I myself never hear that lovely music rising to a tremendous climax without seeing in imagination what was revealed to the Sister of Mercy. I am on a mountain top before dawn; the darkness gives way; the greyness strengthens, and finally my whole mind and soul are filled with the increasing light.

SUPERSTITION

The best definition of superstition that I can remember was made by James Russell Lowell.“ Superstition, by which I mean the respecting of that which we are told to respect rather than that which is respectable in itself.” Mental slavery is always degrading; and superstition is a form of slavery, because the mind is subjected to fear. As Notoriety is the bastard sister of Reputation, so Superstition is the bastard sister of Religion. The difference between the two can be easily and simply expressed, but it is literally all the difference in the world. The most elevating influence known to man is Religion; the least elevating is Superstition.

The instinctive pessimism of humanity is shown in many careless phrases such as “It’s too good to be true.” The majority of men and women believe that hopes are illusory, but fears accurately foretell the coming event. Yet any sensible old man or old woman will tell us that nearly all the fears and worries from which they themselves suffered almost daily during a long life really never materialised. They suffered for nothing. We learn little from their experience, but go on our way filled with apprehension and alarm. Shakespeare said the brave man dies only once, but cowards die a thousand times in fearing death. I suppose most of us are cowards. Although we are still in good enough health to carry on, we have already died of cancer, tuberculosis, and many other diseases.

Many social superstitions were cured by that great turning point in history, the French Revolution. The world has never been quite the same since the year 1789. Before that date, people really believed that those who were born in noble and royal families were superior to the common herd; after that date the nobility still believed it, but the common people did not agree. They found they had been respecting that which they had been told to respect, rather than that which is respectable in itself. A Frenchman remarked, "The great appear to us great because we are kneeling let us rise." In 1789 everybody stood up.

It is foolish to respect any person or any institution unless it is respectable. The religion of many unenlightened people seems to be based largely on fear, in which case it is of course not religion at all, but rank superstition. James Whitcomb Riley told me of a remark made by a small boy to his mother at bedtime. He jumped into bed, and to the question of his mother, "What, aren't you going to say your prayers?" the child answered, "No, I ain't going to say my prayers tonight, and I ain't going to say 'em tomorrow night, nor the next night. And then if nothing happens, I ain't ever going to say 'em again."

This all-too-typical boy looked upon prayer as a means of warding off danger, and he was sufficiently intelligent and sufficiently brave to risk its omission. But if he had been brought up to believe that prayer is neither a charm against peril nor a method of getting what you want, that prayer was intimate communion with a Divine Friend, he would have looked upon it from a different point of view. George Meredith told his son never to ask any material thing from God, but to pray to Him every day of his life.

Now many men and women have the religious maturity of a small boy, which is infinitely worse than having the religion of a little child. They never pray except when they are in danger, or when they think they are going into danger, or when they have suffered from some calamity. That is like speaking to a friend only when you want to borrow money. The profound wisdom of mysticism consists not in making use of God, but in hoping and believing that God will make some use of us.

The base-born idea that God is against us is accompanied by the idea that He may be placated or humoured. In Richard Halliburton's exciting account of his adventures in southern countries, he tells us how the pagan priests used to sacrifice thousands of young maidens to their deity. It would seem, looking back on history, that the more abominable the religion, the fewer the atheists. Every sensible person in those countries ought to have been an atheist.

Now although many "enlightened" people today laugh at the terrible fears and even more terrible remedies of those intellectual slaves, they themselves are not very much wiser. It is highly probable that the majority of Americans today would not dare to say "I haven't had a bad cold this winter" without touching wood. Some of them might grin as they touched it, but they would touch it just the same. Such a gesture is intellectually and morally contemptible.

But many are even poorer in brains. For many would not dare to say that they had not had a cold this winter, with or without wood in reach. They believe that if you express anything pleasant, you will soon "get your comeuppance." God seems to lie in wait for us, and the moment we seem satisfied or happy or even prominent, He will teach us who is running the show. The best thing therefore is never to appear too happy. For many, who have been foolish enough to say aloud, "I haven't had a cold this winter," wake up the next morning snuffling. "Now you see what I've got! If I'd only had sense enough to keep my mouth shut, I would have been all right. But of course I had to brag about it!"

The most degrading of all superstitions is the belief that God can be placated, appeased, or diverted, as we humour a refractory boy or a drunken man. This abominable idea sometimes takes an extremely tragic form, as when the Indian mother throws her own baby into the Ganges. "Now, God, you've got to be good to me! I've given you the best thing I had!"

Sometimes it takes a merely silly form, as when one gives up some pleasant little luxury; not with the great idea of drawing nearer to God by removing an obstacle, but with the absurd idea of bargaining with Him.

TEA

"Thank God," said Sydney Smith, "thank God for tea! What would the world do without tea?-how did it exist? I am glad I was not born before tea." Well, I get along very well without tea, though I rejoice to see that more and more in "big business" houses in American cities there is a fifteen-minute pause for afternoon tea.

One of the chief differences between the life of Englishmen and of Americans is tea. Millions of Englishmen take tea three times a day. Tea is brought to their bedside early in the morning, and thirstily swallowed while in a horizontal attitude. The first thing an Englishman thinks of, if he wakes at dawn, is tea. When Arnold Bennett was travelling in America he took a limited train from New York to Chicago. Early in the morning he rang for the porter and when that individual appeared he commanded nonchalantly a cup of tea. He might as well have asked for a pot of hashish. The porter mechanically remarked that the "diner" would be put on at such-and-such an hour. This unintelligible contribution to the conversation was ignored by the famous novelist, who repeated his demand for tea. He was amazed to find there was no tea. "And you call this a first-class train!" Then at breakfast-a substantial meal in British homes, though having somewhat the air of a cafeteria-tea is drunk copiously. To the average American tea for breakfast is flat and unprofitable. We are accustomed to the most inspiring beverage in the world, actual coffee. The coffee in England is so detestable that when an American tastes it for the first time he thinks it is a mistake. And he is right. It is. Many Americans give it up and reluctantly order tea. In my judgment, for breakfast the worst coffee is better than the best tea.

There are many Americans who have tea served at luncheon. For some reason this seems to the Englishman sacrilegious. The late Professor Mahaffy, who is now (I suppose) drinking nectar, was absolutely horrified to find that in my house he was offered a cup of tea at lunch. "Tea for lunch!" he screamed, and talked about it for the rest of the meal.

I was invited by a charming American lady to meet an English author at her house for luncheon. Tea was served and she said deprecatingly to the British author, "I don't suppose you have tea at this time in England." "Oh, yes," said he, "the servants often have it below stairs." To my delight, the hostess said, "Now, Mr.   , aren't you really ashamed of offering me an insult like that? Isn't that remark of yours exactly the kind of thing you are going to be ashamed of when you think it over, all by yourself?"

At precisely 4:13 p.m. every day the average Englishman has a thirst for the astringent taste of tea. He does not care for hot water or hot lemonade coloured with tea. He likes his tea so strong that to me it has a hairy flavour. Many years ago the famous Scot William Archer invited me to his rooms in the Hotel Belmont, New York, for afternoon tea at 4:15. He had several cups and at five o'clock excused himself, as he had to go out to an American home for tea. I suggested that he had already had it. "Oh, that makes no difference."

There are several good reasons (besides bad coffee) for tea in England. Breakfast is often at nine (the middle of the morning to me), so that early tea is desirable. Dinner is often at eight-thirty, so that afternoon tea is by no means superfluous. Furthermore, of the three hundred and sixty-five days of the year in England, very, very few are warm; and afternoon tea is not only cheerful and sociable but in most British interiors really necessary to start the blood circulating.

There are few more agreeable moments in life than tea in an English country house in winter. It is dark at four o'clock. The family and guests come in from the cold air. The curtains are drawn, the open wood fire is blazing, the people sit down around the table and with a delightful meal-for the most attractive food in England is served at afternoon tea-drink of the cheering beverage.

William Cowper, in the eighteenth century, gave an excellent description:

Now stir the fire and close the shutters fast, Let fall the curtains, wheel the sofa round, And while the bubbling and loud-hissing urn Throws up a steamy column, and the cups That cheer but not inebriate wait on each, So let us welcome peaceful evening in.

Not long before this poem was written the traveller Jonas Hanway had the bad luck to publish an essay on tea, "considered as pernicious to health, obstructing industry, and impoverishing the nation," which naturally drew the artillery fire of the great Dr. Johnson. Sir John Hawk-his, in his life of Johnson, comments on this controversy. He says: "That it is pernicious to health is disputed by physicians"-where have I heard something like that recently? But Hawkins continues: "Bishop Burnet, for many years, drank sixteen large cups of it every morning, and never complained that it did him the least injury."

As for Johnson, "he was a lover of tea to an excess hardly credible; whenever it appeared, he was almost raving, and by his impatience to be served, his incessant calls for those ingredients which make that liquor palatable, and the haste with which he swallowed it down, he seldom failed to make that a fatigue to every one else, which was intended as a general refreshment."

In nearly every English novel I find the expression, "I am dying for my tea!" On a voyage to Alaska, where tea was served on deck every afternoon, at precisely the same moment an elderly British lady appeared from below with precisely the same exclamation: "Oh, is there tea going?" And on her face was a holy look.

Alfred Noyes told me that during the war, when he was writing up important incidents for the benefit of the public, he was assigned to interview the sailors immediately after the tremendous naval battle of Jutland. He found a bluejacket who had been sent aloft and kept there during the fearful engagement, when shells weighing half a ton came hurtling through the air and when ships blew up around him. Thinking he would get a marvellous "story" out of this sailor, Mr. Noyes asked him to describe his sensations during those frightful hours. All the man said was, "Well, of course, I had to miss my tea!"

TEN SIXTY-SIX

All persons who speak the English language should never forget the year 1066, for although it bloomed and faded long ago, it was an important event in our lives. In that year William the Conqueror sailed across the English Channel, landed on the south coast of England, and his descendants and those of his party are there yet.

No wonder the British are proud of their naval and military history. England is separated from the continent by only twenty miles; and yet since 1066 not a single person has got into England and stayed there without an invitation. For nearly nine hundred years England has successfully repelled boarders. Many able and determined foes devoted all their energies to realise their heart's desire. The Spanish Armada was a grandiose war-fleet, but Sir Francis Drake and the surface of the Channel that has made so many tourists seasick, were too powerful a combination for the gallant Spaniards. The dream of Napoleon was to invade and possess England; the nearest he ever got to it was St. Helena. There is an enormous column at Boulogne which was erected to "commemorate the intention of Napoleon to invade England." I knew that intentions were often used as pavingstones in a certain locality; but, like Browning's futile lovers in *The Statue and the Bust,* the immobility of the commemoration is an ironical commentary. In the World War, the Central Powers were well-equipped for an expeditionary force on land, water and air; the best-selling novel in Germany in 1916 was called *General Hindenburg's March into London,* but it was a work of the imagination.

In reading Tennyson's play *Harold,* it is interesting to see that his sympathies are all with the Saxon king; and it is well to remember that William could not have conquered England had not Harold been engaged in a fatal civil war with his own brother Tostig. Was there ever a more suicidal folly? When William landed, Harold was fighting away up in the North in what is now Yorkshire; and he had to bring his army down to the South coast through incredibly bad roads, and there meet the First Soldier of Europe.

However and whatever Tennyson may have thought, William's victory was the best thing that ever happened to England and to those who now speak English. The battle of Hastings meant much to Americans. Not only was William a statesman and law-and-order man, he made English a world language. By the addition of the Romance languages to Anglo-Saxon, he doubled the richness of our vocabulary; English is a gorgeous hash of Teutonic and Latin tongues. But William did far more for us than that. Anglo-Saxon, the language spoken by Harold in London, is more unlike the language spoken by King George V than the language of Virgil in Rome is unlike the language spoken by Mussolini.

Anglo-Saxon is a difficult language, as difficult for a beginner as German; furthermore, it is inflected. William, although he did not know it, made English the universal language, the clearing-house of human speech in the twentieth century.

It is easier for an American to learn either French or German than it is for a German to learn French or a Frenchman to learn German. Not only are there many words in English which are like French words, but the most blessed result of this victory in 1066 was the eventual simplification of English grammar and syntax.

If William had not conquered England, it is probable that today English speech would have inflexions and grammatical gender. George Moore says that he dislikes English, it is a lean language, the adjective does not agree with the noun-I say, thank Heaven for that! With the exception of pronunciation, the English language is ridiculously simple and easy; any foreigner can learn to write, read and understand English in a short time, and he can learn to speak it with fluent inaccuracy. What a blessed thing for a foreigner who must learn English to know that when he learns the name of a thing that name does not change. A book is always a book, no matter what you do with it. Now, if William had not conquered England, every time you did anything to a book, the accursed word would change. "The book is mine," but "I take bookum," "I go away booke," "I tear a page out bookes," and so on. Then one would have to discover and remember whether book were masculine, feminine, or neuter, and every time one used an adjective, like "good book," that miserable adjective would have to agree with the book in gender, case and number. When one sits down to dinner in a German hotel, one must remember that the knife is neuter, the fork is feminine, and the spoon masculine, and then one's troubles have only begun.

Remember what Mark Twain said of German. How simple to have no case-ending, no gender, and almost no grammar ! No wonder English is becoming the world-language; it will of course never drive out other languages, but it has already taken the place occupied by Latin in the Middle Ages, and by French in the eighteenth century. A man can go almost anywhere in the world with English; and any foreigner who decides to learn one language besides his own, must choose English. Anyhow they all do.

The only difficulty with our language is its pronunciation. Not only are we the only people in the world who pronounce the vowels a, e, i, as we do, there are so many exceptions that this rule does not always apply. One has to learn the pronunciation of every word. Suppose a foreigner learns *danger,* what will he do with *anger?* And having finally learned both anger and danger, what will he do with *anger? I* never met but one foreigner who spoke English without a trace of accent; that was the late Professor Beljame, who taught English at the

Sorbonne. He told me that he had practiced English every day for forty years, and I afterward discovered that his mother was an Englishwoman. One day I met a Polish gentleman who spoke English fluently, but with much accent; he insisted that he spoke it as well as a native. I left him alone for three hours with this sentence:

> "Though the tough cough and hiccough plough me
> through"; and when I came to hear him read it,
> I thought he was going to lose his mind.

THE DEVIL

It is rather a pity that the Devil has vanished with Santa Claus and other delectable myths; the universe is more theatrical with a "personal devil" roaming at large, seeking whom he may devour. In the book of Job the Devil played the part of the return of the native, coming along in the best society in the cosmos to appear before the Presence. And when he was asked where he came from, he replied in a devilishly debonair manner, "From going to and fro in the earth, and from walking up and down in it."

There are so many things in this world that seem to be the Devil's handiwork, and there are so many people who look like the devil, that it seems as if he could not be extinct. His chief service to the universal scene was to keep virtue from becoming monotonous; to warn even saints that they must mind their step; to prove that eternal vigilance is the price of safety. The Enemy of Mankind never took a holiday. Homer might nod, but not he. In fact, on human holidays he was, if possible, unusually efficient. The idleness of man was the opportunity of Satan.

The principle of evil is so active, so tireless, so penetrating that the simplest way to account for it is to suppose that men and things receive constantly the personal attention of the Devil.

Weeds, and not vegetables, grow naturally; illness, not health, is contagious; children and day-labourers are not instinctively industrious; champagne tastes better than cocoa.

Throughout the Middle Ages, although every one believed steadfastly in the reality of the Devil and that he was the most unscrupulous of all foes, there was a certain friendliness with him, born, I suppose, of daily intimacy. It was like the way in which hostile sentries will hobnob with one another, swap tobacco, etc., in the less tense moments of war. The Devil was always just around the corner and would be glad of an invitation to drop in.

Thus in the mediaeval mystery plays, the forerunners of our modern theatres, the Devil was always the Clown. He supplied "comic relief" and was usually the most popular personage in the performance. He appeared in the conventional makeup, a horrible mask, horns, cloven hoofs and prehensile tail, with smoke issuing from mouth, ears and posterior. He did all kinds of acrobatic feats, and his appearance was greeted with shouts of joy. In front of that part of the stage representing Hellmouth he was sometimes accompanied with "damned souls," persons wearing black tights with yellow stripes. On an examination at Yale I set the question, "Describe the costume of the characters in the mystery plays." One of the students wrote: "The damned souls wore Princeton colours."

The modern circus clown comes straight from the Devil. When you see him stumble and fall all over himself, whirl his cap aloft and catch it on his head, distract the attention of the spectators away from the gymnasts to his own antics, he is doing exactly what his ancestor the Devil did in the mediaeval plays.

It is at first thought singular that those audiences, who believed implicity in a literal hell of burning flame, should have taken the Devil as the chief comic character. I suppose the only way to account for this is to remember how essential a feature of romantic art is the element of the grotesque, which is a mingling of horror and humour, like our modern spook plays. If you pretend that you are a hobgoblin and chase a child, the child will flee in real terror, but the moment you stop, the child will say, "Do that again."

There are many legends of compacts with the Devil, where some individual has sold his soul to gain the whole world. The most famous of these stories is, of course, Faust, but there are innumerable others. Here is a story I read in an American magazine some fifty years ago.

A man, threatened with financial ruin, was sitting in his library when the maid brought in a visiting card and announced that a gentleman would like to be admitted. On the card was engraved Mr. Apollo Lyon.

As the man looked at it his eyes blurred, the two words ran together, so they seemed to form the one word Apollyon.

The gentleman was shown in; he was exquisitely dressed and was evidently a suave man of the world. He proposed that the one receiving him should have prosperity and happiness for twenty years. Then Mr. Lyon would call again and be asked three questions. If he failed to answer any of the three the man should keep his wealth and prosperity. If all three were correctly answered the man must accompany Mr. Lyon.

The terms were accepted; all went well for twenty years. At the appointed time appeared Mr. Lyon, who had not aged in the least; he was the same smiling, polished gentleman. He was asked a question that had floored all the theologians. Mr. Lyon answered it without hesitation. The second question had stumped all the philosophers, but it had no difficulties for Mr. Lyon.

Then there was a pause, and the sweat stood out on the questioner's face. At that moment his wife came in from shopping. She was rosy and cheerful. After being introduced to Mr. Lyon she noticed her husband was nervous. He denied this, but said that he and Mr. Lyon were playing a little game of three questions and he did not want to lose. She asked permission to put the third question and in desperation her husband consented. She held out her new hat and asked: "Mr.

Lyon, which is the front end of this hat?" Mr. Lyon turned it around and around, and then with a strange exclamation went straight through the ceiling, leaving behind him a strong smell of sulphur.

THE FORSYTE SAGA

It is impossible to say what books of our time will be read at the close of this century; it is probable that many of the poems and tales of Kipling, the lyrics of Housman, dramatic narratives by Masefield, some plays by Shaw and Barrie, will for a long time survive their authors.

Among the novels, I do not know of any that has or ought to have a better chance for the future than the books written about the family of the Forsytes by John Galsworthy. They at present hold about the same place in contemporary English literature as is held in France by Romain Rolland's *Jean Christophe.* Both are works of great length which reflect with remarkable accuracy the political, social, commercial, artistic life and activity of the twentieth century, the one in England, the other on the Continent.

Entirely apart from their appeal as good novels, that is to say, apart from one's natural interest in the plot and in the characters, both are social documents of great value. If the future historian wishes to know English and Continental society in the first quarter of the twentieth century, he will do well to give attention and reflexion to these two works of "fiction."

John Galsworthy was just under forty when in 1906 he published a novel called *The Man of Property*. He had produced very little before this, but it took no especial critical penetration to discover that the new book was a masterpiece. The family of the Forsytes bore a striking resemblance to one another in basic traits and ways of thinking, yet each was sharply individualised.

A new group of persons had been added to British fiction. The word "Property," as in Tennyson's *Northern Farmer*, was the keynote, and before long it began to appear that one of the most dramatic of contrasts was to be used as the subject. This is the struggle between the idea of Property and the idea of Beauty-between the commercial, acquisitive temperament and the more detached, but equally passionate artistic temperament.

Even in the pursuit of beauty Mr. Soames Forsyte never forgot the idea of property. He was a first-class business man in the city, but he was also an expert judge of paintings, which he added to his collection. Oil and canvas do not completely satisfy any healthy business man; so Soames added to his collection, as the masterpiece in his gallery, an exquisitely beautiful woman whom he made his wife.

The philosophy of love comes in here. What is love? Is it exclusively the idea of possession, which often is no more dignified than the predatory instinct or is it the unalloyed wish that the object of one's love should be as happy and secure as possible? No one can truly and sincerely love Beauty either in the abstract or in the concrete if one's eyes are clouded by predatory desire. One must look at beauty without the wish to possess it if one is really to appreciate beauty. A first-class French chef would look into the big front window of a confectioner's shop and fully appreciate the art and taste that created those delectable edibles; but a hungry boy who looked at the same objects would not appreciate them critically at all.

The wife of Soames finds him odious, so odious that we cannot altogether acquit her of guilt in marrying him; and Soames, who as a Man of Property expected her to fulfill her contract, did not make himself more physically attractive by insisting on his rights. She left him for a man of exactly the opposite temperament.

When Mr. Galsworthy finished this fine novel, he had no intention of going on with the history of the family. He wrote many other novels and some remarkable plays, but nothing made the impression on readers that had been produced by the Forsyte family. Nearly twenty years later he returned to the theme, and at once his power as a novelist seemed to rise; there is something in this family that calls out his highest powers. When he discovered that he had written five works of fiction on the Forsytes, three long novels and two short stories, of which the brief interlude called *Indian Summer of a Forsyte* is an impeccable and I hope imperishable work of art, he hit upon the happy idea of assembling them into one prose epic, and calling the whole thing by the ironical title of *The Forsyte Saga.* It is my belief that for many years to come the name of John Galsworthy will be associated with this work, in what I fervently hope will be its expanded form.

For since the assembling of the five pieces Mr. Galsworthy has published several other novels dealing with the family. -*The* 1,T% *hite Monkey, The Silver Spoon* and in 1928 he wrote FINIS with Swan *Song.* Here he kills Soames, and while he probably does not feel quite so sad as Thackeray felt when he killed Colonel Newcome, I venture to say that he does not gaze on the corpse of Soames with indifferent eyes. For to my mind the most interesting single feature of this whole mighty epic is the development of the character of this man.

Clyde Fitch used to say something that is no doubt true of many works of the imagination; he said that he would carefully plan a play, write his first act, and definitely decide what the leading characters should say and do in the subsequent portions of the work. Then these provokingly independent characters seemed to acquire, not only an independent existence, but a power of will so strong that they insisted on doing and saying all kinds of things which he tried in vain to prevent.

In *The Man of Property* Soames Forsyte is a repulsive character; he is hated by his wife, by the reader, and by the author. But in these later books Soames becomes almost an admirable person, and we may say of him at the end in reviewing his life, that nothing became him like the leaving of it-for he died nobly. Long before this catastrophe, however, we have learned to admire, respect, and almost to love Soames. Is it possible that Mr. Galsworthy had any notion of this spiritual progress when he wrote *The Man of Property*, or is it that in living so long with Soames he began to see his good points?

Dickens was a master in this kind of development. When we first meet Mr. Pickwick, he seems like the president of a service club as conceived by Sinclair Lewis; he is the butt of the whole company. Later Mr. Pickwick develops into a noble and maganimous gentleman, whom every right-minded person loves. Look at Dick Swiveller-when we first see him, he is no more than a guttersnipe. He develops into a true knight.

THE GREAT AMERICAN GAME

Baseball is American in its origin, development and area. It is also American in its dynamic qualities of speed and force, and in the shortness of time required to play a full game and reach a decision. Americans do not love serial games like cricket; in literature they are better at writing short stories than at novels, and they enjoy games where a verdict is soon reached.

Looking back over the history of this national pastime, I can remember when the pitcher was allowed nine balls before losing his man, and one year in the last century it took four strikes to retire the batsman. I can also remember when a foul ball caught on the first bound was "out," when a foul tip-often successfully imitated by clever catchers-was "out," and I played the game many years before an uncaught foul was a strike. In order to have a wider radius for fouls, the catcher used to stand far back, moving up behind the bat only after the second strike, or when bases had the tenancy of opponents. Every advance in the rules has been in the direction of speed; and at present the game seems unimprovable.

Nearly every game has some inherent defect; as putting is sixty-five per cent of golf, so pitching is sixty-five per cent of baseball. Moral: Be a good putter, and see that your nine has a good pitcher.

Pitching seems to be a greater physical and mental strain than in the last century, although the box artist does not pitch so many balls in the average game as he used to. In spite of that fact, Radbourne of Providence, who was the greatest professional pitcher I ever saw, won the national championship for his team in 1884 by pitching every day for a long period. And his team-mate, the late John M. Ward, who afterwards joined New York, told me that in 1879 he pitched sixty-six consecutive games! The universal disease of nerves, from which no twentieth century American is exempt, is probably responsible for the more careful treatment of pitchers today.

On July 23, 1884, the Providence club, then in the National league, was crippled for pitchers. Radbourne went into the box from that date until September 26 when he had won the National league pennant, daily, except August 2, 18, 20. He pitched thirty-six games during that period, twenty-two on consecutive days, and winning eighteen. Of the thirty-six, he won thirty-one, lost four, and tied one.

Tim Keefe in 1888 broke Radbourne's record for straight games won, by winning nineteen, and Marquard in 1912 equalled Keefe's. Next to Radbourne comes Joe Wood, with sixteen straight, won in 1912.

Radbourne's total feat for the 1884 season of pitching seventy-seven games (seventy-four National league championships and three world series, winning three straight in the world series -no other pitcher was used) is another record that stands.

The greatest baseball player of all time is Tyrus Raymond Cobb, of Georgia. He not only holds an unexampled batting record, his speed in the outfield was so great that he was moved from right to centre, and in his baserunning it is not much to say that he raised the art to a higher plane. Ordinarily, the best of players was content to steal second, but if Cobb saw that the ball was not going to beat him to the second bag, he kept right on to third. The bewildered second baseman, who naturally had a psychological caesura when the attempted play failed, had to begin all over again in order to catch his parting guest at third. And, flustered as he was by the sheer audacity of the thing, he was apt to be wild Cobb capitalised his reputation; he knew the basemen were all "laying for him," and owing to that curse which has always afflicted humanity, which makes it more difficult to do a thing in proportion to one's desire to do it, they found it more of a task to retire Cobb than to retire anyone else. If they had not known it was Cobb, they could have got him. Mr. Cobb told me once that it was largely a matter of mind reading; he had to out-guess his opponents, he had to know what they were going to do.

Certainly his stealing of bases has been phenomenal; he would steal first base if he could. His ambitious, fiery, high-strung disposition, which is largely responsible for his success, has also caused him to lose his temper on the field. This is regrettable, and of course, must be punished. And yet I have some sympathy for these lapses, and do not condemn them unqualifiedly as some colder judges do. The anxiety to win is what enrages a player when things go wrong, and I fully understand it though I recognise its sinfulness. Although I myself was very carefully brought up by a pious father and mother, and although I had the unspeakable advantage of being a Yale graduate, I once threw a bat at an umpire when he called me out on strikes. In order to atone for this sin, I have often-like Doctor Johnson-stood unprotected in the rain, when I had no umbrella.

The greatest baseball pitcher in Yale's history was Amos Alonzo Stagg, of the class of 1888. He won the championship over both Harvard and Princeton five successive years, pitching in every championship game. He headed the batting order, was a fine base-runner, and in minor games, played behind the bat, on the bases and in the outfield. He knew baseball thoroughly. He never had great speed, or wide curves; but he had marvellous control and a memory that was uncanny. If a batsman faced him once, Stagg never forgot him, and thereafter never gave that batsman anything he wanted.

Carter, of the class of '95, was a great pitcher and all-round ball player, as different in other respects from Stagg as could well be imagined. Stagg was very short; Carter was six foot four. Carter had blinding speed with tremendous curves. But if you compare his record of championships with that of his predecessor, you will see why I rate him second to Stagg. These two men, are, I think, Yale's foremost box heroes.

Baseball is not so spectacular as football, but in one respect it has a great advantage over its more lusty rival. Everyone sees what happens in baseball; the spectator sees every play, and he knows instantly the reason for every success and every failure. In football the ball is concealed in the line, very few can see exactly what has happened, and no one knows whether a run or a touchdown is going to count or not, until the official has given his consent; and if he withholds his approval, and the ball is brought back, the spectators do not know why.

THE GREATEST COMMON DIVISOR

Some distinguished novelists are like lofty peaks. Few ascend them and those who do breathe rarefied air. There are writers whose fame is apparently secure who have never had many readers, and there are writers who have an enormous public and no fame. George Meredith and Henry James were men of genius, and there will always be enough people of taste to save some of their books from oblivion; but neither of these authors made much money. Both Meredith and James would have liked to have a million readers; perhaps it is to their credit that they made no compromises to increase the sales of their works, perhaps they could not have succeeded in such an undertaking had they tried.

While in the long run it is popularity that determines a writer's fame-not only Shakespeare, but every first rate English poet has today many thousands of readers-there are also "trashy" books which sell like gasolene, and there are trashy books which do not sell at all. It is a comforting thought that the majority of trashy books have a smaller sale than masterpieces, and that the best book ever written has had, has, and will have the largest sale of all.

It won't do to prefer posterity to popularity; posterity is more cruel to the average writer than are his contemporaries.

Shakespeare was the most popular Elizabethan dramatist; Ben Jonson, the foremost press agent of his time, said that his friend Shakespeare had surpassed all the writers of Greece and Rome, which was exactly what John Dryden, the foremost press agent of his time, said of his contemporary, Milton. Gray's *Elegy,* Byron's *Childe Harold,* Tennyson's In *Memoriam,* Kipling's *Rece*ssional, were popular two weeks after their publication, and they are popular now.

In the long run the best books have the largest sales. In every age, however, there are certain novelists of prodigious vogue, whose works nevertheless are to readers of good taste negligible. The common people read them gladly and the Scribes and Pharisees regard them with scorn. When our high school teachers and junior college professors wish to relieve their systems of accumulated bile, they pour out before their sceptical pupils bitter denunciations of Harold Bell Wright, the late Gene Stratton Porter and Zane Grey. They try to persuade their flocks that the books by these writers are not interesting; but the flocks know that they are, and instead of despising these novelists, they lose confidence in their instructors.

Far be it from me to pretend that Mr. Wright and Mr. Grey are literary artists, or to enter the lists as a champion of their works. What I have read of them has not left me with an insatiable appetite for more. But here is a fact of interest to students of books and of human nature-of the "works" of Porter and of Wright over nine million copies have been sold, and as we rate five readers to every copy, each of these two worthies has an audience of forty-five million readers. What does this mean? Many will say it means that the public loves trash. I don't believe it; the majority of books are trash, and the majority of books do not sell. Some critics and some unsuccessful writers say that they could write just the same sort of thing if they would stoop to it; I don't believe it. The financial rewards of popularity are so great that many writers would produce tales of adventure if they were sure of a million readers.

It is possible that boys and girls read these books because of their good qualities rather than because of their defects. Why is it that these authors are Greatest Common Divisors? Why do they make the largest appeal to the largest number of people?

Well, in the first place they are novelists, and the foremost of recent novelists, Thomas Hardy, says that the novel should tell a story. The average school-boy knows that a book by Wright, Porter or Grey will have a good story. The majority of our novelists either will not or can not tell a story. All they have is a time plot, beginning with the smells the baby had in his cradle, of no interest to any one except the novelist, going on with his fights and loves at school, etc., etc. Most people are like the Sultan in the Arabian Nights, they love a good story; Wight, Porter and Grey furnish it. The lives of most boys and girls are not romantic or unusual; in the novel they get an escape from life, a change of air, a vacation; and there is nothing boys love more than a vacation. Again, however deficient in conduct boys and girls may be, they instinctively love courage, honour, truth, beauty, magnanimity; the novels of the Terrible Three all work for righteousness. In the eternal conflict between good and evil, these Greatest Common Divisors are on the right side; even if they do not know much about style, or much about psychology, or much about subtlety of motive, they do know the difference between right and wrong, something that some much be praised novelists seem to have forgotten or to think unimportant.

I do not believe the majority of supercilious critics and other cultivated mature readers began in early youth by reading great books exclusively; I think they read *Jack Harkaway,* and *Old Sleuth,* and the works of Oliver Optic and Horatio Alger. From these enchanters they learned a thing of importance-the delight of reading. Once having learned that having found that a book, easily procurable, is the key to happy recreation, they obtained a never-failing resource of happiness.

A similar thing is observable in poetry. If a boy learns to love highly exciting narrative poetry, or pretty sentiments set to easy tunes, it is more probable that he will later love great poetry than if he never caught the lilt of words in youth.

Nothing that I have said is at variance with one of my oft-expressed beliefs-those parents who are not only interested in the welfare of their children, but are capable of setting them a good example, do not need to use the Greatest Common Divisor so often. They can by sympathetic intercourse with their children, and by patience, bring them up from the start on the Bible, Shakespeare, Bunyan, Swift, Defoe and other writers of genius; but a large number of boys and girls come to our schools from uncultivated homes, and from parents who are stupid, or selfish, or silly; these children must learn the magic of books, and it is my belief that the makers of exciting stories, with sentiment laid on thick, with heroes and heroines who are brave, honourable and virtuous are performing a public service.

THE IMPORTANCE OF THE EARTH

Perhaps nothing nowadays is a more common target for ridicule than the hustler and booster, whether he boosts as an individual or as a member of a service organisation. The man whose motto is "bigger and better business," a bigger town, with a bigger population and bigger buildings, is laughed at for his enuthusiasm and for his perspiring efforts. Much of this laughter is merely the cynical adverse criticism of men who have never done anything themselves, never will do anything, and so pretend to be faintly and superciliously amused by the optimistic exertions of others. We may dismiss these unproductive and complacent occupiers of the seats of the scornful, for they are comparatively few in number and their opinions of no moment. But the rational basis for laughter at the booster is that the hustler and the booster often have a false standard of excellence.

When a noisy man roars in your face that the population of his particular town has doubled in ten years we have a right to enquire, what of it? Is it a cause for rejoicing? When you climb into a trolley car on a rainy day you do not rejoice because the population of the trolley car doubles in three minutes. A mere increase in the number of persons at a given spot does not necessarily mean that collectively or individually they are any better off. What we wish to know is something quite different from the word "more." Is the community growing in intelligence? Are there better schools, better theatres, better art museums, better churches, better orchestras-are the inhabitants of this locality growing in grace and in the fruits of the spirit?

The last thing I wish to be guilty of is to make cheap remarks against science or scientific men to whom I, in common with others, owe so much; but, strangely enough, some of the professional men of science, who are often the first to laugh at the booster because he applies the quantitative rather than the qualitative standard of measurement, are themselves guilty of the same fault on a larger scale. They do not apply standards of size to a growing business or a growing village; they apply these standards to the universe.

Now, as is well known, the Ptolemaic system of cosmogony stated that the earth was the centre of the universe and that around the earth revolved the sun, the moon and all the innumerable stars. Thus man regarded himself as of high importance because he was the centre of everything.

Along came Copernicus, whose book was published in 1543 but not generally accepted until long after its appearance. Copernicus wrought a far greater miracle than Joshua. The Old Testament hero made the sun stand still only for an afternoon; but in the sixteenth century Copernicus commanded the sun to stand still and (relatively speaking) it has not budged since. Copernicus was a magician.

Many astronomers have recently been fond of reminding us that our sun itself is only a tiny star-one out of many billions-and that our earth is but the tiniest speck. They are fond of drawing diagrams showing the comparative size of our sun and that of other globes in the starry skies, and the earth dwindles to a mere point. "Therefore," say these scientists, "how unimportant is man and how ridiculous that he should consider either himself or his earthly abode a matter of any importance to God or to space or time or gravitation"; the conclusion following that religion and morals are matters of small consequence and we need not bother our heads about them.

Now it seems to me that expressions of this kind are as fallacious and as injurious as any booster's standard of mere quantity; for what are these gentlemen trying to say except that as the earth is so tiny in comparison with other stars it must necessarily follow that man himself is a very unimportant factor in the universe? On the contrary, I believe the earth to be the most important spot in the entire creation and that the most precious thing on the earth is man-men, women and children.

The ordinary ignoramus looks at the starry vault and exclaims: "There are all those stars and every one inhabited with life!" As a matter of fact the latest researches of science show that the rarest thing in the entire universe is human life. There is not one vestige of evidence to show that life exists anywhere except on the earth.

The universe is frightfully hot. The fixed stars have a temperature ranging from nearly two thousand degrees to more than thirty thousand degrees, which is considerably hotter than the Needles in California. Furthermore, among all the heavenly bodies *planets* are the most scarce, and the only conditions which can produce a planet occur almost never. Now the planets in our particular little solar system had the good luck to come into being, and of these planets only the earth can support human life. The late Percival Lowell, an eminent astronomer and a gallant gentleman, looking at the sky through the clear air of Arizona, thought he saw evidence of the intelligent work of beings on Mars, but he saw it because his telescope was not good enough; "bigger and better" telescopes destroyed the illusory things he thought he saw.

I advise all those who believe in the insignificance of man because he lives on a small ball to read the last chapter of Sir James Jeans's book *The Universe Around Us.* Sir James does not himself say that man has a divine destiny, because that is not the subject of his book. But he does say: "All this suggests that only an infinitesimally small corner of the universe can be in the least suited to form an abode of life."

People used to be flabbergasted by the consideration of the vastness of the starry heavens while retaining their respect for man and their own self-respect; but of late years many astronomers, by applying the "big and little" method of measurement, have tried to convince us that man is of no importance. Thus astronomy, instead of filling its students with majestic wonder, fills them with despair. To these scientific boosters it is the devout and not the undevout astronomer who is mad.

Fear not, little flock. We are no longer the geographical centre of the universe, but--so far as evidence goes-we are the only part of it that amounts to anything.

THE INCOME TAX

There are many people who believe that an income tax is bound to come in America, and await its appearance with that dull resignation characteristic of the attitude of the ultimate consumer toward our lawmakers in Congress assembled. Like sheep led to the shearers they are dumb, while the professional politicians open their mouths. This curious and revolutionary scheme of taking money away from those who have earned it is discussed usually only by legislators and economists; the vast number of those who will have to pay are not considered qualified even to have an opinion, much less to utter it in public. But it might be interesting to consider the effect of the income tax on that huge class of Americans, who are neither poor nor rich, but are just able to support their families on a fixed salary or a fairly regular income. The man on a steady salary does not seem to gain directly during seasons of great national prosperity. He finds his income the same, with its purchasing power considerably decreased. If he were forced to pay, in addition to his living expenses (which already make it impossible for hits to save anything but his life insurance), a section of his salary to the national government every year, he would find it necessary to give up, not the luxuries of life, but same of the things his wife and children regard as necessities. He should be pardoned if he does nut welcome the idea of a national income tax with enthusiasm. Suppose his income were four thousand dollars, with the cost of living steadily increasing. This figure would make it certain that if the income tax slid not hit him on its first imposition I use the ward in all its senses it would on the second or third amendment. Fortunately, his moral character would not suffer, for any temptation to conceal from the taxgatherer the exact amount of his receipts would be overcome by the known impossibility of success. It is quite easy for the inquisitor to discover the exact income of a man on a fixed salary.

The income tax is a great feature of life in England, where the proposition seemed originally not only feasible, but desirable; there being no protective tariff, it was thought that the poor and those of moderate means could buy the necessities of life cheaply in the world's cheapest market, while the rich could support the government out of their superfluous incomes. At first the tax was imposed only on large incomes, and only a small percentage had to be paid in; but naturally enough, with the increasing expenses of national budgets, the range of the tax was steadily widened to cover moderate incomes, and the amount of the tax increased as well. Now every one who has an annual income of $700 must pay the tax, and the percentage is so great that, what with local rates plus the income tax, many Englishmen are forced to pay in taxes seven shillings in every pound, or a little more than one-third of their entire income.

Persons, therefore, of moderate "leans are having a desperate struggle to pay the tax and live, while the condition of the very poor has not improved at all. There is no country in the world that has been more torn by strikes and labor troubles during the past two years than Great Britain. The reason is that it is impossible under the present condition of affairs in England to give workingmen high wages; and the absence of protective tariff has very little effect the price of food, which is the big item in every poor man's expenses. The Poor in England do not receive enough wages to buy a sufficient amount of good food, and the manufactories, railways and employers in general cannot afford to pay them much more than they now receive. Hence, constant strikes, struggles and universal discontent, with the black shadow of revolution.

The Englishmen of moderate means with whom I have spoken are not very keen in their support of the income tax as a means of national revenue. They are hard hit.

Altho I do not care to discuss the income tax as a political measure, and have nothing but contempt for the cheap demagogery of some of its advocates, it seems to me somewhat strange that either of our great political parties should have coquetted with such a scheme. From the point of view of Federal control, the determination to centralize as much power as possible in the Government at Washington, to the exclusion of the rights of the separate States, it might be a logical plank in the platform of the Republicans-, but on the other hand, the Republicans have always set their faces against direct taxation, believing that the easiest way to raise all the immense expenses of the national government is by high impost duties. All taxes are odious; even the most patriotic citizens do not overvalue their property, except when they wish to sell it, nor do they greet the arrival of a tax bill with a shout of joy. But the least odious way to pay taxes is when they are indirect; when all luxuries and some necessaries cost a little more than they would without an impost. Thus, for the Republican party to abandon the indirect system of taxation for the direct would be a right-about-face in party tradition and party policy.

But this is nothing compared with the situation from the Democratic point of view. The historic position of the Democratic party, and to my way of thinking, its finest attitude as an organization, is its old and firm belief in local self-government. Historically, the party resists strenuously any attempt on the part of the Federal Government to assume powers that belong to the States or to interfere with the rights of individuals as citizens in States. Everyone, by a little effort of memory can recall the rage of the Democrats some twenty years ago, when it was proposed by the Republicans to pass a Federal Elections bill, which meant that national elections in the States should be under the supervision of Federal officers. Southern gentlemen dubbed this Republican partisan measure the "Force bill," and they fought it with fury, and finally succeeded in talking it to death in the Senate. The idea of a Federal officer at a Southern polling station was to them intolerable, and they were quite right, it seemed to me, in their fierce opposition. But now we see many good Southern Democrats cheerfully voting to sanction the visit of a Federal officer into every Southern home, an inquisitor who has the right to ask the most personal questions as to the source, nature and amount of every individual's earnings. This has a humor all its own, for not only is the State's sacred right of taxation to be surrendered, but the privacy of every individual is to be invaded by a Federal officer. I suppose some of the Democratic enthusiasm for this arbitrary and dangerous power to be given to the Federal Government is caused by the belief that more Republicans than Democrats will have to pay the piper. But let no man deceive himself. Even if this thing starts as a rich man's tax it will soon cease to be such, and the weight of it will eventually fall on the great army of men and women who have only moderate means, where it may become a burden well nigh intolerable. And if in the future the Republicans should once again endeavor to establish Federal control of State elections, the Southerners who have voted to bring Federal officers into Southern homes would find it difficult to assume their former attitude of pious horror. Nothing is more dangerous than to surrender personal liberty and local self-government into the hands of a centralized force.

In England, every man or woman who owns a little stock receives the dividend shorn of the income tax. The tax is first taken out and the stockholder gets what is left. How will this proposition be greeted by the vast number of people in America who own only a few shares?

I refrain from speaking of the enormous expense necessary to collect this tax, of the amount of fraud and lying that it will cause, for the reasons given above are sufficient to condemn so unAmerican, so inquisitive and so odious a scheme of taxation.

THE POETRY OF WALT WHITMAN

Editor's Note

THE material contained in this book is a reprint of the second essay in the volume by William Lyon Phelps, entitled "Howells, James, Bryant and Other Essays."

The Poetry of Walt Whitman LOOKING over some Whitman manuscripts in the library of Yale University, I found a letter from the poet, which is so characteristic that I place it here at the head of this essay

The Poetry of Walt Whitman

Camden, Oct. 14, 1880. Dear Tom: I got home all safe- We stopped a day & a night at Niagara & had a first rate time-- Started the next morning early in an easy comfortable palace car & went on like a streak through New York & Pennsylvania-got into Philadelphia after 11 at night-(we were an hour late)-but the city looked bright & all alive. O I felt as fresh as a lark-I am well, my summer in Canada has done me great good-it is not only the fine country & climate there, but I found such good friends, good quarters, good grub, & every thing that could make a man happy-The last five days I have been down on a jaunt to the sea-shore. . . I sat hours enjoying it, for it suits me-I was born & brought up near the sea, & I could listen forever to the hoarse music of the surf-Tom I got your paper & handbill, good for you, boy-believe me I was pleased to know you won.

Whitman was always cheerful, always the optimist, always the affirmer of life, and the believer in it. He regarded mere animal existence as a huge asset, and conscious living as a continuous joy.

He had as little of Mark Twain's pessimism as of his humour; the only point where these representative Americans came in contact was their faith in the universal principle of Democracy.

Who is America's foremost poet? It would be impossible to obtain a majority on a secret ballot for any one. Poe, Emerson, Longfellow, Whittier, Lowell, Whitman have many supporters. Our most popular poet is of course Longfellow; but the greatest? I cannot tell. Emerson and Whitman are the most unconventional, the most free of tradition.

John Burroughs, the faithful disciple of old Walt, divided all poets into two classes-Primary and Secondary. He declared emphatically that Whitman was a greater poet than Tennyson, because Tennyson was a secondary man, and Whitman was primary. He meant that Tennyson followed in broad highways, whereas Whitman blazed a trail. However this may be, I do not believe that Whitman was a greater poet than Tennyson, for the simple reason that his poetry is not so good as Tennyson's.

Yet the reputation of Walt Whitman was never so high as it is now. There were two American centenaries in the year 1919; homage was paid to Lowell and to Whitman. But the latter poet was more widely and more vigorously applauded. There are still many sceptics, many avowed antagonists; but we shall never be rid of him. We cannot say, as some tried to say of a greater poet with the same initials, William Wordsworth, Here lies W. W.

Who no more will trouble you, trouble you, for Whitman will trouble us to the end of our lives, and cannot be dismissed with a Podsnappian gesture.

The history of his reputation demands a volume by itself. It began with Leaves of Grass, in 1855. That was a notable year in poetry, for it saw also the appearance of Tennyson's Maud, Browning's Men and Women, Longfellow's Hiawatha. Maud and Hiawatha received much ridicule, and Men and Women received silence. Today all these poems are very much alive.

Whitman's admiration of other poets was sufficiently eclectic. His roll-call of the "mighty ones" is as follows: Job, Homer, zEschylus, Dante, Shakespeare, Tennyson, Emerson.

What I shall say about Whitman will please nobody; for I am neither among the worshippers nor the scorners. To me he is neither one-of-the-greatest-poets-of-all-time nor is he a charlatan. I refuse to become excited or polemical in this matter. Whitman needs no defence and attacks cannot hurt him.

It was during the 'seventies that the battle raged most fiercely. To some enthusiasts, Whitman was in the front row with Homer and Shakespeare; to other men he was an unclean boor who should be summarily expelled into the outer darkness. Just when the fight was hottest, an obscure young Scot by the name of Robert Louis Stevenson published an essay called The Gospel According to Walt Whitman (1878) which in 1923 seems still to be the best appraisal. Let me quote the first paragraph

Of late years the name of Walt Whitman has been a good deal bandied about in books and magazines. It has become familiar both in good and ill repute. His works have been largely bespattered with praise by his admirers, and cruelly mauled and mangled by irreverent enemies. Now, whether his poetry is good or bad as poetry, is a matter that may admit of a difference of opinion without alienating those who differ. We could not keep the peace with a man who should put forward claims to taste and yet depreciate the choruses in Samson Agonistes; but I think we may shake hands with one who sees no more in Walt Whitman's volume from a literary point of view, than a farrago of incompetent essays in a wrong direction. That may not be at all our own opinion. We may think that, when a work contains so many unforgetable phrases, it cannot be altogether devoid of literary merit. We may even see passages of a high poetry here and there among its eccentric contents.

But when all is said, Walt Whitman is neither a Milton nor a Shakespeare; to appreciate his works is not a condition necessary to salvation; and I would not disinherit a son upon the question, nor even think much the worse of a critic, for I should always have an idea what he meant.

Whitman was born on a farm in Long Island, 31 May 1819. He was the second of nine children, and was called "Walt" to distinguish him from his father Walter. He was the only one of the brood to show any ability. Bliss Perry says the oldest died a lunatic and the youngest was an imbecile.

When he was four years old, the family moved to Brooklyn. Walt had little formal education; at the age of 13, he left school "for good." He did much desultory reading, set type in a printing office, did editorial writing on the Brooklyn Eagle, and taught school. This last experience he valued highly. The best thing he got out of his newspaper work was free admission to the New York theatres; he was a constant attendant at plays and operas. Like most men of force and vigour, he loved to read the Bible, and was particularly fond of reading it outdoors, which is one of the severest tests that can be applied to any book. He knocked around the South as a jolly vagabond, doing odd jobs in New Orleans and other places. During the Civil War, he did noble and devoted service in taking care of the sick and wounded in the hospitals. He had everlasting patience, reading to the men, and writing letters for them, listening to their talk and telling them stories. In 1873 paralysis seized him. His declining years were spent at Camden, New Jersey. Friends supported him, and he thoroughly enjoyed life, sending copies of his own books to purchasers, composing and revising, receiving daily visits from idolaters and pilgrims who came from everywhere. He became a Sage, and his particular Boswell, Horace Traubel, has left a voluminous and detailed record of his conversations. He died on 26 March 1892.

All of Whitman's unconventionalities, in dress, name, and literary style, were deliberately assumed. They were not spontaneous. As a young man, he was something of a macaroni. He dressed in formal and elaborate style, with a frock coat, tall silk hat, and carried a cane. Later he wore a grey flannel shirt, open at the neck, with rolling Byronic collar. In each case he meant to be conspicuous, and succeeded. Originally he signed his work Walter Whitman, and later changed to Walt, as more free-and-easy. His literary career began in an extremely conventional manner; his first publications were in prose, his enemies insist that his later ones were also. When he wrote his first poems, they were written in a correct, conventional, traditional, uninspired metrical form. Probably no famous writer ever made more revolutionary changes in his mental attitude towards life and art.

At the age of twenty-three, Whitman made his first appearance as an author. In a periodical called The New World, New York, November 1842, there appeared what was described as an "original temperance novel,"

FRANKLIN EVANS: OR, THE INEBRIATE A Tale of the Times by WALTER WHITMAN

This is written in an insufferable style, stilted, sophomoric, melodramatic, sentimental, turgid, impossible. It sounds like a burlesque on a temperance tract, but it was serious. T. S. Arthur's Ten Nights in a Bar-room, a hot favourite with children, is mild and restrained in comparison with Franklin Evans: The Inebriate.

In 1850, in a miscellany called Voices from the Press, appeared a short story by Whitman, with the fantastic title, The Tomb Blossoms. Here the country is praised in contrast to the city, a strange point of view when we remember Crossing Brooklyn Ferry. The style of this tale is no better than that of its predecessor.

Meanwhile, Whitman was studying verse-forms and casting about for something by which to attract the attention of the public. For whether he was a genius or a faker, one thing is certain. Never was there a man who so loved publicity. The limelight was as necessary to his personal comfort as water is to a fish. He could not endure obscurity.

Bliss Perry, in his Life of Whitman, has pointed out the remarkable similarity between a free-verse poem, The Lily and the Bee, by Samuel Warren, published in 1851, and the style of Leaves of Grass, 1855. It is impossible to avoid the conclusion, that although Whitman did not borrow from Warren, he had read him with profit. The rhythmic prose of the Bible and the rhapsodical pages of Ossian had been familiar to Whitman since childhood. Evidently he feared that Leaves of Grass might be called an imitation of Ossian, for in the notes that he wrote for his own guidance, we find "Don't fall into the Ossianic by any chance."

When Leaves of Grass appeared in 1855, Whitman hoped that it would make a sensation-that it would either be greeted as the work of a new and authentic prophet, or that it would become a public scandal. To his dismay, it fell flat, and attracted hardly any attention. He therefore wrote long and laudatory reviews of it, which appeared anonymously in various periodicals. But even these puffs failed to start a fire.

Whitman sent out presentation copies to distinguished men, and in one instance the result was magnificent. On 21 July

1855, Emerson wrote a glowing and generous letter, that filled the new poet with natural and justifiable exultation. Here are some of the phrases in which Emerson expressed his recognition and tribute.

"I find it the most extraordinary piece of wit and wisdom that America has yet contributed. I am very happy in reading it, as great power makes us happy. I find incomparable things, said incomparably well, as they must be. I greet you at the beginning of a great career."

This last phrase, Whitman, without asking permission, placed in letters of gold, signed R. W. Emerson, on the outside of the cover of the new edition in 1856, which gave the philosopher the severest test of his tranquillity that he had ever been forced to meet.

Many short reviews of the book consigned it to the garbage-heap, and some insisted that the author should be arrested. Thus there began that fierce quarrel about Leaves of Grass that will never be completely and finally settled. The reason is simple enough; there are poems of amazing originality and beauty, and there are passages which never should have been printed. Whitman was a man of genius; but he had no humour, no taste, and no sense of proportion. On this whole question young Mr. Stevenson, in 1878, said the last word:

In his desire to accept all facts, facts loyally and simply, it fell within his programme to speak at some length and with some plainness on what is, for I really do not know what reason, the most delicate of subjects. Seeing in that one of the most serious and interesting parts of life, he was aggrieved that it should be looked upon as ridiculous or shameful. No one speaks of maternity with his tongue in his cheek; and Whitman made a bold push to set the sanctity of fatherhood beside the sanctity of motherhood, and introduce this also among the things that can be spoken of without a blush or a wink. But the Philistines have been too strong; and, to say truth, Whitman has rather played the fool. We may be thoroughly conscious that his end is improving; that it would be a good thing if a window were opened on these close privacies of life; that on this subject as on all others, he now and then lets fall a pregnant saying. But we are not satisfied. We feel that he was not the man for so difficult an enterprise. He loses our sympathy in the character of a poet by attracting too much of our attention in that of a Bull in a China Shop. And where, by a little more art, we might have been solemnized ourselves, it is too often Whitman himself alone who is solemn in the face of an audience somewhat indecorously amused.

In dismissing this subject, there is no doubt that Whitman was sincere. But there is also no doubt that his chronic itch for publicity made him more daring than would otherwise have been the case. Since we know how intensely he loved to attract attention, that the chief delight in his life was to be talked about, it is as certain as anything can be that he deliberately put in passages which he believed would make a sensation. They certainly eventually helped to sell his book; they help to sell it now. Emerson pleaded with him in vain; Whitman insisted that nothing should be struck out, and that no abridged version of his poems should appear. Shortly before his death, he finally consented to the publication of a volume of Selected Poems, chosen with great skill by Arthur Stedman, who said in his preface, "This edition of Mr. Whitman's poems is, on his part, a concession to friendship.

He has not abandoned his position, but has yielded to urgent request." Mr. Stedman did the old poet a valuable service. Those who had heard of Whitman only as a charlatan or as an immoral writer, found in this little volume of Selections enough authentic poetry to change their attitude.

It was not long before parodies appeared, for the subject invited that form of criticism which can best be expressed in parody and burlesque. Whoever is interested in this branch of Whitmaniae, may now be referred to a book published in 1923, called Parodies on Walt Whitman, edited by Henry S. Saunders, with a disarming preface by Christopher Morley. The parodies begin with the year 1857, and close with 1921. Most of them do not seem nearly so funny to us as they must have seemed to their authors. The times have changed, and

Whitman is an accepted poet. His peculiarities are so well known that the parody now fails of its intended effect. The best one in the book, as might be expected, is that by the late H. C. Bunner.

The reason why, with a few exceptions like Emerson, Leaves of Grass was received either with silence or with abuse, was because of its unlikeness to conventional poetry. When genius supplies a demand, as in the instances of Byron and Tennyson, immediate popularity is the result. There has always been, there is now, and there always will be, a sharp demand for beautifully melodious poetry. But where Genius has to create the demand as well as the supply, where the new forms or the new treatment are entirely unlike what the world is looking for, then the way towards recognition is difficult. Original genius is outside of the law of supply and demand. There was no demand for Browning, or for Ibsen, or for Wagner, or for Whitman; these four men had to create the demand as well as the supply. The mass of people are conventional, like schoolboys, and they distrust and often hate anything that is unconventional or even unusual. What first impressed the public in the works of these Four was not its greatness, but its strangeness; that quality of strangeness had to overcome the natural opposition and inertia of humanity, before the greatness could be recognised. For the conventional public opinion, as expressed in print hundreds of times on these four men, was, that whatever they might be, they were assuredly not what they professed to be. Ibsen was not a dramatist; Wagner was not a musician; Browning and Whitman were not poets.

How fortunate it was for these four that they all lived to be old! Had they died in middle life, they would have died unrecognised. But Wagner, Ibsen, Browning, and Whitman received in old age the tribute of universal fame, which must have been all the sweeter for having been long deferred.

Yet although Whitman died a famous poet, his reputation then was nothing to what it is now. In the 'nineties, the controlling voice in English poetry was Rudyard Kipling, who was as unlike Whitman as could be imagined. Kipling had vitality, originality, and force; but he expressed himself carefully in conventional metres. The whole tendency of verse in both England and in America then seemed towards more rather than less restraint in form; the most popular poet in America, James Whitcomb Riley, was conventional metrically. He despised Whitman and all his works.

Furthermore, although Whitman's admirers insisted that he was the voice of democracy, the common people never heard him gladly. The average Americans read Longfellow and Whittier, because those poets best expressed their own inarticulate feelings; they knew little about Whitman and cared less. He, the poet of democracy, was read chiefly by a few literary aristocrats in Europe and in America, whose jaded taste required something new.

But owing to the renaissance of poetry which began in Europe and in America a few years before the Great War, and was definitely stimulated by that catastrophe, the general public began to read Whitman, and for the first time, he became a popular poet. Again, a renaissance of poetry necessarily means experimentation; and during the last ten years many young poets are avowed followers of Whitman, both in writing free verse, and in their fondness for new forms of expression. In a word, Whitman has come into his own.

It is perhaps natural that in the nineteenth century Whitman had more admirers in Europe than in America. He was regarded as the poet of Democracy, America's authentic voice. We, who lived in the atmosphere and environment which he tried to express, would not naturally have been so impressed as those dwelling afar off. Europeans have always been trying to find some one who should reveal the American spirit, and many thought the search was rewarded in Leaves of Grass.

When discussion of Whitman became common in England, there arose the same violent difference of opinion as was evident here. Dante Rossetti, in a letter to William Allingham in April 1856, wrote, "I have not been so happy in loathing anything for a long while-except, I think, Leaves of Grass, by that Orson of yours. I should like just to have the writing of a valentine to him in one of the reviews." Later, in 1878, in commenting on his brother's Lives of Famous Poets, Dante Rossetti said: "I am sorry to see that name winding up a summary of great poets." The two brothers never agreed about this, for in 1869, William Michael Rossetti wrote, "That glorious man Whitman will one day be known as one of the greatest sons of Earth, a few steps below Shakespeare on the throne of immortality."

Swinburne's opinion about Whitman suffered a curious change. When he first read Leaves of Grass, shortly after its appearance, he was enthusiastic and spoke highly of it. Even as late as 1885 he wrote, "I retain a very cordial admiration for not a little of Whitman's earlier work." But in 1887 Swinburne made a thorough recantation, saying that Whitman's Muse was a "drunken apple-woman, indecently sprawling in the slush and garbage of the gutter amid the rotten refuse of her overturned fruit-stall."

In America, Dartmouth College can claim the honour of being the first academic institution to treat Whitman officially with respect. He was invited to deliver the Commencement Poem in 1872, and he accepted, writing and reading on that occasion a poem originally called As a Strong Bird on Pinions Free. In the Complete Works this title was changed to Thou Mother with Thy Equal Brood. In the same year of its delivery he published the Dartmouth poem, with a preface so important, and made even more so by the years 1914-1918, that it is necessary to quote from it.

The impetus and ideas urging me, for some years past, to an utterance, or attempt at utterance, of New World songs, and an epic of Democracy, having already had their publish'd expression, as well as I can expect to give it, in "Leaves of Grass," the present and any future pieces from me are really but the surplusage forming after that volume, or the wake eddying behind it. I fulfill'd in that an imperious conviction, and the commands of my nature as total and irresistible as those which make the sea flow, or the globe revolve. But of this supplementary volume, I confess

I am not so certain. Having from early manhood abandon'd the business pursuits and applications usual in my time and country, and obediently yielded myself up ever since to the impetus mention'd, and to the work of expressing those ideas, it may be that mere habit has got dominion of me, when there is no real need of saying anything further. But what is life but an experiment? and mortality but an exercise? with reference to results beyond. And so shall my poems be. If incomplete here, and superfluous there, n'importe-the earnest trial and persistent exploration shall at least be mine, and other success failing shall be success enough. I have been more anxious, anyhow, to suggest the songs of vital endeavour and manly evolution, and furnish something for races of outdoor athletes, than to make perfect rhymes, or reign in the parlours. I ventur'd from the beginning my own way, taking chances-and would keep on venturing.

I will therefore not conceal from any persons, known or unknown to me, who take an interest in the matter, that I have the ambition of devoting yet a few years to poetic composition. The mighty present age! To absorb and express in poetry, anything of it-of its world-Americacities and States-the years, the events of our Nineteenth century-the rapidity of movementthe violent contrasts, fluctuations of light and shade, of hope, and fear-the entire revolution made by science in the poetic method-these great new underlying facts and new ideas rushing and spreading everywhere; truly a mighty age! As if in some colossal drama, acted again like those of old under the open sun, the Nations of our time, and all the characteristics of Civilization, seem hurrying, stalking across, flitting from wing to wing, gathering, closing up, towards some longprepared, most tremendous denouement. Not to conclude the infinite scenes of the race's life and toil and happiness and sorrow, but haply that the boards be cleared from oldest, worst incumbrances, accumulations, and Man resume the eternal play anew, and under happier, free, auspices. To me, the United States are important because in this colossal drama they are unquestionably designated for the leading parts, for many a century to come. In them history and humanity seem to seek to culminate. Our broad areas are even now the busy theatre of plots, passions, interest, and suspended problems, compared to which the intrigues of the past of Europe, the wars of dynasties, the scope of kings and kingdoms, and even the development of peoples, as hitherto, exhibit scales of measurement comparatively narrow and trivial. And on these areas of ours, as on a stage, sooner or later, something like an eclaircissement of all the past civilization of Europe and Asia is probably to be evolved.

The leading parts. Not to be acted, emulated here, by us again, that role till now foremost in history-not to become a conqueror nation, or to achieve the glory of mere military, or diplomatic, or commercial superiority-but to become the grand producing land of nobler men and women -of copious races, cheerful, healthy, tolerant, free-to become the most friendly nation (the United States, indeed)-the modern composite nation, form'd from all, with room for all, welcoming all immigrants-accepting the work of our own interior development, as the work fitly filling ages and ages to come;-the leading nation of peace, but neither ignorant nor incapable of being the leading nation of war; not the man's nation only, but the woman's nation-a land of splendid mothers, daughters, sisters, wives.

The Four Years' War is over-and in the peaceful, strong, exciting, fresh occasions of to-day, and of the future, that strange, sad war is hurrying even now to be forgotten. The camp, the drill, the lines of sentries, the prisons, the hospitals-(ah! the hospitals!)-all have passed away-all seem now like a dream. A new race, a young and lusty generation, already sweeps in with oceanic currents, obliterating the war, and all its scars, its mounded graves, and all its reminiscences of hatred, conflict, death. So let it be obliterated. I say the life of the present and the future makes undeniable demands upon us each and all, south, north, east, west.

To help put the United States (even if only in imagination) hand in hand, in one unbroken circle in a chant-to rouse them to the unprecedented grandeur of the part they are to play, and are even now playing-to the thought of their great future, and the attitude conform'd to it-especially their great esthetic, moral, scientific future (of which their vulgar material and political present is but as the preparatory tuning of instruments by an orchestra), these, as hitherto, are still, for me, among my hopes, ambitions.

How far and in what sense is Whitman an original writer? It is often stated that he is one of our most original thinkers and poets. His leading ideas are not original. He expresses chiefly enthusiasm for humanity, love of the race, the worship of democracy; all this is emphatically and at times impressively uttered. But it can be found in Rousseau, and has been more poetically expressed by Shelley. Has then Whitman nothing new or important to tell us?

He says "Rejoice in yourselves: in life: in all your bodily functions." Had he proclaimed this some centuries earlier, he might have been called original. The revolt against asceticism, the refusal to regard the human body as vile, the unwillingness to consider human life on earth as a mere vestibule to eternitythese are fundamental ideas in Whitman. But he was by no means the first to proclaim them.

I should say that Whitman was more unconventional than original. As he discarded fashionable clothing, so he discarded fashionable opinions. In America he was more "different" than he would have seemed in Europe. Here he was against the Puritan tradition, against what was understood and agreed upon as decency, against small-town mentality, against any and all reserve. His manners shocked Americans as they could not have shocked Europeans; for example, he was forever kissing men, which simply "isn't done" in America. I remember when a European pianist played in Boston, he was entertained after the concert by an exclusive club. He caused a sensation by insisting on kissing every one of the men who were presented to him. It took them a long while to recover.

Much of the shock caused by Whitman's poetry really had

more to do with literary etiquette than with thought. It was largely a question of manners. Now the older a civilisation is, the freer and franker the behaviour and conversation of the people. In the nineteenth century, things were discussed in books and at dinner-tables on the Continent which were never mentioned in America. And what is true of an old country as compared with a new is true of a large city as compared with a village. Country bumpkins will snigger secretly over vulgarities; but village society says limb when it means leg; prefers circumlocutions to direct statements; and still prefers rhetorical oratory to simple plain language. It is the last citadel of the oldfashioned spell-binder.

In the same way, old countries are more tolerant of religious and political heresies than new ones; and in any country, there is more freedom of speech in a big city than in a village. During and after the Great War, there was more individual freedom of speech in England than in America; and in America, there was more freedom in New York than anywhere else, much more than in country villages. Many were surprised that the penaltiestwenty years in prison, for examplethat were given to persons who expressed heretical political opinions in America were unknown in England; this is really natural, and is simply a register of intellectual levels. We had and have the small-town view, that cannot comprehend opinions contrary to those current in the village.

Whitman's lack of reserve on all topics and his unconventionalities were startling in America in 1855.

In one respect he had the wisdom of the great poets. He was never an opportunist; he did not deal with "timely" questions. Though intensely American, as a poet he was universal and dealt with universal and unchangeable things like human passions and the stars. He was a revolutionist in art, but he was never a political revolutionist; he was not a socialist, not an anarchist, not a political reformer. He was kept from all this not only by his intense individualism, which would have made it impossible for him to cooperate with any organisation, but by a kind of instinctive wisdom, which made him deal with fundamental and eternal things, the true subjects of art.

Whitman's religion was certainly not Christianity, except in one important aspect, his belief in the brotherhood of man. Not only was he devoid even of a grain of Christian faith, he was definitely in opposition to Christian teaching. If I understand Christianity at all, it is opposed to human instincts; it proposes to substitue unselfishness for selfishness, modesty for greed, purity for sensuality, giving for taking, self-control for selfassertion. The reason why Christianity is so unpopular at the present moment-for unpopular it certainly is-is not because it is opposed to reason, for it is in harmony with the only reasonable way of life. It is unpopular because it places a constant veto on human instincts, and we are living

(1923) in a post-war relaxation and hatred of all restraint. Possibly one reason why Christianity has never been popular in any period with the younger generation is because early in life instinct is stronger than reason; wisdom comes, if at all, by experience. Christianity is of course a positive, not a negative religion; it is a religion to live by, not to die by; but, as Browning said, it teaches original sin, the corruption of man's heart. Christianity never uses palliatives or surface remedies; it calls for regeneration, for a new birth, for a complete change in emphasis.

Keats said in one of his letters, "O for a life of sensations rather than of thoughts!" Whitman is more of a sensationalist than a thinker. The tentacles of his mind were all feelers; he was like an AEolian harp, to be played upon by the chance winds of heaven. To regard him as a profound philosopher, prophet, or great teacher is idle; he shows us how to enjoy life, how to appreciate beauty, how to become ever more sensitive to impressions, but he very seldom stimulates the mind. Professor Henry A. Beers is very near the final truth about him, when he says, "If a large, good-natured, clean, healthy animal could write poetry, it would write such poetry as the Leaves of Grass. It would tell how good it is to lie and bask in the warm sun; to stand in cool, flowing water, to be naked in the fresh air; to troop with friendly companions and to embrace one's mate."

One of the reasons why Whitman is so popular at this moment is because many of our novelists and men of letters have substituted the animal for the spiritual attitude towards life. We used to be told that we should conquer the beast in us; now we are told every day to imitate the animals, to be like them, do what we please, and never on any account be sorry afterwards. There are many prominent writers to-day to whom the word sin is obsolete. They are, consciously or unconsciously, followers of Whitman. I cannot imagine old Walt suffering from anything like remorse.

So far as he had a religion, he can be described by the well-known phrase, "cosmic emotion," concerning which Professor W. K. Clifford wrote an interesting essay. Man must have some religion or some substitute for religion; I do not believe the average human being can live without it. If all theistic belief is dead, the religion of nature remains. One goes out at night, contemplates the stars, and feels oneself a part of the universe. To Whitman this was always a solemnizing thought. "The huge and thoughtful night." He was sincere in what religion he had. When a dying soldier asked Whitman to read him a chapter in the New Testament, he read the account of the crucifixion. "The poor, wasted young man ask'd me to read the following chapter also, how Christ rose again. I read very slowly, for Oscar was feeble. It pleased him very much, yet the tears were in his eyes. He ask'd me if I enjoyed religion.

I said, `Perhaps not, my dear, in the way you mean, and yet, maybe, it is the same thing.' He said, `It is my chief reliance.' He talk'd of death, and said he did not fear it."

Whitman was a careful student of rhythm, and had read the Bible to advantage. His best lines have superb rolling music that needs no rime, although he did not disdain rime. His most famous poem is also the most conventional in metre, "O Captain, My Captain." Whitman became tired of hearing this praised, both because he did not wish to be regarded as a man of one poem, and because it was so unlike his more characteristic work. When some one praised it one day, he exclaimed angrily, "Oh, damn My Captain!" His impatience is easy to understand. We are told that a man voted against Aristides because he was tired of hearing him called The Just, but think how utterly weary Aristides himself must have been.

I hold no brief for free verse; other things being equal, I prefer regular metrical forms. But there are certain subjects, which, if Whitman had described them in sonnets, could not have been so impressively brought to our perceptions as Whitman brings them with his irregularities. Take the lines he wrote in Platte Canon, Colorado.

Spirit that form'd this scene,These tumbled rock-piles grim and red,These reckless heaven-ambitious peaks, These gorges, turbulent-clear streams, this naked freshness,

These formless wild arrays, for reasons of their own,

I know thee, savage spirit-we have communed together,

Mine too such wild arrays, for reasons of their own;

Was't charged against my chants they had forgotten art?

To fuse within themselves its rules precise and delicatesse?

The lyrist's measur'd beat, the wrought-out temple's grace-column and polish'd arch forgot?

But thou that revelest here-spirit that form'd this scene,

They have remembered thee.Although Whitman has an unassailable place in literature, and although he has profoundly influenced many young poets, and at no time more than now, his own method-free verse-has not yet given birth to anything supreme. The best free-verse writing in the English language is still to be found in Whitman, and not in the works of his imitators or followers. They have done well, but not supremely well; and their best is below the best conventional work done by their contemporaries. Whitman was undoubtedly a great poet; but who are the leading English poets of the twentieth century? Kipling, Thompson, Phillips, Housman, Henley, Hardy, Hodgson, De La Mare, Noyes, Masefield, Watson, Brooke, Flecker, Davies; and in America, our three leading living poets are Robinson, Lindsay, and Frost. Neither in

England nor in America are the leaders distinguished for free verse composition, but rather for the opposite. Therefore the old battle-cry, that Whitman's is "the poetry of the future," seems particularly untrue.

There are still those who would deny Whitman the rank of great poet. But we should remember that the Republic of Letters is not a social club; genius cannot be blackballed, and Whitman was a man of genius. He often expressed a universal idea in a permanently beautiful phrase. His greatness, indeed, consists not so much in whole poems as in phrases. He had a particular talent for first lines and titles, so that the Table of Contents or Index of First Lines to Whitman's Complete Poems would seem full of promise to one who should stumble on the book without previous knowledge. Like some grocers, he put the best apples on top. Looking down the Table of Contents, one feels that the Table itself is a Poem.

In Cabin'd Ships at Sea I Hear America Singing Shut not Your Doors to Me, Proud Libraries Out of the Rolling Ocean the Crowd

Once I Pass'd Through a Populous CityI Heard You Solemn-Sweet Pipes of the Organ When I Heard at the Close of the Day

I Saw in Louisiana a Live-Oak Growing This Moment Yearning and Thoughtful Fast-Anchored Eternal O Love

O You Whom I Often and Silently Come Song of the Open Road

Song of the Redwood Tree Song of the Rolling Earth Youth, Day, Old Age, and Night Pioneers! O Pioneers!

Out of the Cradle Endlessly Rocking As I Ebb'd With the Ocean of Life To the Man-of-War Bird

The World Below the Brine On the Beach at Night Alone

Song for All Seas, All ShipsWhen I Heard the Learn'd Astronomer The Dalliance of the Eagles

Beat! Beat! Drums!From Paumanok Starting I Fly Like a Bird Song of the Banner at Daybreak

Rise O Days from Your Fathomless Deeps Cavalry Crossing a Ford

By the Bivouac's Fitful FlameVigil Strange I Kept on the Field One NightA Sight in Camp in the Daybreak Gray and Dim As Toilsome I wander'd Virginia's Woods

Year that Trembled and Reel'd Beneath Me Give Me the Splendid Silent Sun

Over the Carnage Rose Prophetic a Voice I Saw Old General at Bay

Ethiopia Saluting the Colors O Tan-Faced Prairie-Boy Look Down Fair Moon

When Lilacs Last in the Dooryard Bloom'd O Captain, My Captain

Hush'd be the Camps To-day By Blue Ontario's Shore There was a Child Went Forth The Singer in the Prison Warble for Lilac-Time

O Star of FranceAn Old Man's Thought of School Proud Music of the Storm Prayer of Columbus

Darest Thou Now O Soul

Yet, Yet, Ye Downcast Hours As if a Phantom Caress'd Me That Music Always Round Me A Noiseless Patient Spider

Thou Mother with Thy Equal Brood Thou Orb Aloft Full-Dazzling

The Mystic TrumpeterTo a Locomotive in WinterAh Poverties, Wincings, and Sulky Retreats Weave in, My Hardy Life

By Broad Potomac's Shore From Far Dakota's Canons Spirit That Form'd this Scene As I Walk These Broad Majestic Days The Sobbing of the Bells

Joy, Shipmate, Joy Sands at Seventy Good-By, My FancyThe art of poetry is an art of expression; we are all poets at heart.

We all have imagination and poetic thought, else why should we find in the great poets so clear an echo of ourselves? The more distinct the echo, the greater the poet. But we are inarticulate; we cannot express ourselves; we love music, and we cannot sing. The great poets are the spokesmen for humanity. Whitman spoke out for us all. There are passages in such poems as Columbus, When Lilacs Last, The Man-of-War Bird, that rhythmically sing thoughts that are universal.

Furthermore, there is something healthy in his optimism. He was never petulant, never cynical, never despairing. To him Life was good. He belongs not among those who have despised the supreme gift of life, not among the deniers, but among the Affirmers. He was entirely free from the prevailing modern disease, the fear of life. He loved life, and welcomed experience; he was devoid of fear. He calls upon us to rejoice; to use our eyes and our senses; to commune in rapture with the sea and the stars.

In a certain sense, Whitman interpreted America to Europe; and to America he tried to interpret the universe.

The End

THE WEATHER

Nearly all the great poetry of the world, ancient and modern, has been written in Europe. This fact should never be forgotten in reading literature that alludes to the weather. The reason every one talks about the weather is not that the average person has nothing else to say; it is that the weather is usually the most interesting topic available. It is the first thing we think of in the hour of waking; it affects our plans, projects and temperament.

When I was a little boy at school there was a song sung in unison called "Hail, Autumn, Jovial Fellow!" It seemed to me to express correctly the true character of autumn. It was not until I had reached maturity in years that I discovered that the song, as judged by the world's most famous writers, was a misfit. Instead of autumn's being jovial, it was dull, damp, dark, depressing. To be sure, I never really felt that way about it; the evidence of my eyes was in favour of the school song, but, as the great poets had given autumn a bad reputation, I supposed in some way she must have earned it.

Still later I learned that Goethe was right when he said that in order to understand a poet you must personally visit the country where he wrote. Literary geography is seldom taught or seriously considered, but it is impossible to read famous authors intelligently without knowing their climatic and geographical environment. So keenly did I come to feel about this that I finally prepared a cardboard map of England, marking only the literary places, and I required my students to become familiar with it. One of them subsequently wrote me a magnificent testimonial, which I have often considered printing on the margin of the map.

Dear Mr. Phelps-I have been bicycling all over England this summer, and have found your Literary Map immensely useful. I have carried it inside my shirt, and I think on several occasions it has saved me from an attack of pneumonia.

There are millions of boys and girls studying Shakespeare in South Africa, Australia and New Zealand; the poet's frequent allusions to the climate and the weather must seem strange. That you have such a February face.

February "down under" is midsummer.

Southern latitudes give the lie to Shakespeare's metaphors.

The reason autumn has so bad a name in the world's poetry and prose is that autumn in Northern Europe is a miserable season. In London, Paris, Berlin, November (and often October) is one of the worst times of the year. A chronically overcast sky, a continual drizzle, a damp chill even on mistily rainless days, combine to produce gloom.

The first autumn and winter I spent in Paris revised my notions of those two seasons. As an American, I had thought of the difference between summer and winter as a difference only in temperature; I reasonably expected as much sunshine in autumn and winter as in summer. A typical January day in New York is cold and cloudless. Well, in Paris the sun disappeared for weeks at a time, and on the rare occasions when it shone people ran out in the street to look at it. One of the worst jokes in the world is the expression, "sunny France." The French themselves know better. Frangois Coppee wrote of the "rare smiles" of the Norman climate, and Anatole France, describing a pretty girl, wrote "Her eyes were grey; the grey of the Paris sky."

For the same reason "Italian skies" have been overpraised, because their eulogists are English or French or German. The Italian sky is usually so much better than the sky of more northerly European localities that it seems good by contrast. Now, as a matter of fact the winter sky over Bridgeport, Conn., is superior in brightness and blueness to the sky over Florence or Venice.

November, one of the best months of the year in America, is dreaded by all who live in France, England or Germany. Walking in New Haven one brilliant (and quite typical) day in midNovember, exhibiting the university and city to a visiting French professor, I enquired, "What do you think of our November climate?" He replied, "It is crazy."

A strange thing is that Bryant, born in the glorious Berkshires of western Massachusetts, where autumn, instead of being pale and wet as the European poets have described it, is brilliant and inspiring, all blue and gold, did not use his eyes; he followed the English poetical tradition.

The melancholy days are come, the saddest of the year. James Whitcomb Riley used the evidence of his senses, and wrote an autumnal masterpiece.

0 it's then's the times a feller is a-feelin' at his best . . .

They's something kind o' hearty-like about the atmosphere

When the heat of summer's over and the coolin' fall is here-

Of course we miss the flowers, and the blossoms on the trees,

And the mumble of the hummin'-birds and buzzin' of the bees;

But the air's so appetizin'; and the landscape through the haze

Of a crisp and sunny morning of the airly autumn days
Is a picture that no painter has the colorin' to mock
When the frost is on the punkin and the fodder's in the shock.

One difference between the temperament of the typical

Englishman and the typical American is caused largely by the climate, and foreigners in writing books about us should not forget the fact. If nearly every morning the sky were overcast and the air filled with drizzle, we might not be quite so enthusiastic.

On the other hand, the early spring in England and France is more inspiring than ours, perhaps by reason of the darkness of winter. It comes much earlier. Alfred Housman says:

> Loveliest of trees, the cherry now
> Is hung with bloom along the bough,
>
> And stands about the woodland ride
>
> Wearing white for Eastertide.
>
> In our Northern American States a blossoming fruit tree at Eastertide would be a strange spectacle.

WAR

War is a sentimental affair; that is why it is so difficult to abolish. War is opposed to the dictates of common sense, prudence, rationality, and wisdom. But the sentiments of man and the passions of man are deeper, more elemental, and more primitive than his intelligence, knowledge, and reasoning powers. For intelligence and morality belong to man alone; his instincts he shares with the entire animal creation.

My own plan for getting rid of war would not win a peace prize, because it would never be adopted. But I believe it strikes at the root of war-sentiment. My plan would be to spoil the good looks of the officers and also take away all their drums, fifes, and brass bands. The uniforms are altogether too handsome, too attractive, too becoming.

It is a familiar saying that every woman is in love with a uniform; to which I would add that every man is also. The naval officers look magnificent in their bright blue frock coats, their yellow buttons, and their shining epaulets. These gorgeous hawks of war are decorated by the government as lavishly as Nature, the greatest of all tailors, fits out her birds of prey. A naval officer excels in brilliance the appearance of a civilian, even as the gay feathers of a sparrowhawk excel those of a sparrow.

Furthermbre, every military and naval officer has a capable man to look after his wardrobe. Not only are his various uniforms beautiful in design and ornamentation, they are without spot or blemish. His trousers are mathematically creased, his coat unwrinkled, his linen like virgin snow. My suggestion is, that if you really want to get rid of war, the first thing to do is to compel all professional warriors to wear ill-fitting handme-downs, shabby and unpressed, and without gold trimmings. The glamour and the glory would vanish with the gold.

Then I would abolish the dance of death. Instead of having perfect drill, hundreds of men deploying with exactitude, I would make them look like Coxey's Army, every man for himself, and the devil take the hindmost.

But above all, I would silence the drum and fife, and the big brass band. Although I myself hate war, and should like to see it abolished, whenever I hear the thrilling roll of the drums and the shrill scream of the fifes, followed by the sight and sound of marching men, their bayonets gleaming in the sunshine, I want to cry. A lump comes up in my throat and I am ready to fight anybody or anything. If you really want to get rid of war, you must not surround it with pomp and majesty, you must not give it such a chance at our hearts.

Although wars are never started by warriors, but only by politicians and tradesmen, for the very last place where a foreign war could begin would be at Annapolis or West Point; still, there is no doubt that high officers have a ripping time during a great war, and that the surviving soldiers love to talk about it (among themselves) at their regular reunions in later years. Shakespeare, himself no soldier, understood perfectly how the professional feels. This is the farewell he put in the mouth of Othello:

> Farewell the tranquil mind: farewell content!
>
> Farewell the plumed troop and the big wars
>
> That make ambition virtue!
>
> 0, farewell! Farewell the neighing steed, and the shrill trump,
>
> The spirit-stirring drum, the ear-piercing fife,
>
> The royal banner, and all quality,
>
> Pride, pomp, and circumstance of glorious war!

Even so: Othello was a sentimentalist. He had more passion than brains. That is why Iago and not Desdemona made him jealous; that is why, with the loss of war and women, he lost everything. He was without any intellectual resources.

The leaders of thought and the leaders of morals have usually been against war. Although the historical books of the Old Testament and the emotional Psalms celebrated the glory of war, the contemporary sober-minded prophets were against it. They prophesied the coming of universal peace, when the money spent on armaments would be devoted to agriculture and to education. The appearance of Jesus was the signal for peace on earth and good will to men.

Jonathan Swift, more than two hundred years ago, said that men were less intelligent than beasts. A single wild beast would fight for his food or his mate; but you could never, said Swift, induce a lot of wild beasts to line up in dress parade, and then fight another set of wild beasts, whom they did not know.

Benjamin Franklin, the wisest of Americans, immediately after the Revolutionary War, which he had helped to win, said there had never been a good war or a bad peace.

But although the wisdom and morality of mankind have been against war, war goes on; the moment it breaks out in any country, all the forces of sentimentalism are employed to glorify, yes, even to sanctify its course. The first great casualty is Reason.

What shall we say of a scholar like the late Sir Walter Raleigh, Professor of English Literature at Oxford? He continually ridiculed religion for its sentimentality; but the moment the great war broke out, no school-girl was more sentimental than he.

Thus the hope for peace lies not in the poets, the literary men, the preachers and the philanthropists; the hope lies in hardheaded Scotsmen like Ramsay MacDonald, whose idealism is built on a foundation of shrewd sense.

WHAT THE MAN WILL WEAR

Men, women, and children are all interested in clothes; there have been many scholarly works, displaying vast erudition, on the history of costume; and two literary masterpieces, dealing with the philosophy of clothes, belong permanently to literature-A *Tale of a Tub,* by Jonathan Swift, and *Sartor Resartus,* by Thomas Carlyle.

So much attention has recently been paid in the newspapers and by the public to the clothes of women, that we are forgetting what revolutionary changes have taken place in the garments of men. Women's clothes have decreased in number, weight, and size. Men's clothes have gone through a process of *softening.* Hard hats, hard collars, hard shirts, hard shoes, hard suits, have given way to soft; and, for the first time in centuries, the carcasses of males are comfortably clad.

One hundred years ago the average gentleman, not satisfied with covering his body with an accumulation of intolerably thick clothes, wound an enormous stock around his neck. How stifling they look in those old family portraits! Robert Louis Stevenson applied an unexpected but accurate adjective to those collections of oil paintings of deceased ancestors, with which their descendants adorned walls of their dining rooms. Stevenson called them "these constipated portraits."

This is the way my father dressed on practically every morning of his life; that is, after he left the farm, and entered upon the practice of his profession. He wore long, heavy flannel underwear, reaching to his ankles and his wrists. He put on a "hard-boiled," white, full-bosomed shirt, stiff as sheet-iron. At the neck he fastened a stiff, upright, white linen choker collar; at the ends of the sleeves he buttoned on thick, three-ply linen cuffs. He imprisoned his feet, ankles, and shins in black, stiff, leather boots, reaching to the knees, but concealed above the ankles by his trousers. He wore a long-tailed coat, a waistcoat, and trousers made out of thick, dark-blue or black broadcloth. The trousers were strapped over his shoulders by suspenders. For the top of his head there was a tall, heavy, beaver hat.

Thus, clad in impenetrable armour from head to foot, he set out for the day's work.

Fifty years ago was the age of dressing-gown and slippers. Why is it we never hear slippers mentioned nowadays? I have not owned a pair of slippers (except bedroom slippers) for more than thirty years. Yet in Victorian novels we are always reading of how, when the breadwinner returns to his home in the evening, he finds his slippers ready for him, warmed on the hearth. My father always took off his great boots-worn in summer as well as in winterand put on his slippers when he came home, having called it a day.

Poets, novelists, and men whose occupation kept them at home, sat down to their desk in dressing-gown and slippers. The moment a man sat down in his own house to anything, with no immediate thought of going out, dressinggown and slippers were the regulation costume. They were like knights-at-arms, taking off their suits of mail when they entered the interior of the castle.

Eventually the knee-boots gave way to high shoes-called boots in England-which were laced up to the top. In time these were succeeded by low shoes, which are now worn by millions of Americans the year round.

The swaddling, stiffing, heavy underclothes were scrapped, and their place taken by sleeveless, shinless undergarments, light in weight, and more or less open in texture. Best of all, the intolerable stiff shirt, the bottom edge of which cut into the abdomen, and bellied out above like a sail in a fair wind, was reserved only for formal evening wear; shirts were made and worn that had no trace of starch in front, back, collar or cuff. I have not worn a stiff shirt (except for evening) in twenty years.

Suspenders (braces) became obsolete; and the pleasant belt came in, the belt that may be loosened or tightened at will, and which in any case leaves the shoulders free. In hot weather the waistcoat was discarded; and the man in his thin, loose clothes moved about almost as easily as Adam in Paradise.

Various are the names for the round stiff hat, derby, dicer, pot hat, bowler, billy-cock. Under any name it is just as bad. Some fifteen or twenty years ago the derby went temporarily out of fashion. Up to that time, if you looked into a cloak-room by a hotel dining-room, you saw about two hundred men's hats looking exactly alike. Now you see a vast assortment of soft headgear, grey, brown, green, all of pleasing shape. The thousands of men at a football game now show variety aloft, instead of the intolerable black monotony of former years. I have not owned a "derby" since the war. Apart from my own hatred of the object, I always crushed it getting in or out of an automobile. And one indentation ruins a derby forever: every wound is mortal.

I am quite aware that the derby is returning. Everyone knows the nation-wide fame acquired by a certain brown derby. But no stiff hat, black or brown, will ever adorn my brows again during the hours of daylight.

The English, owing to their horrible climate and also partly to an invincible conservatism, still wear heavy clothes, thicksoled high shoes, braces, waistcoats, etc., even in hot weather. The only reform they have made is discarding the frock coat for daily wear, which up to a very few years ago was universal. A common sight in London was to see clerks going to the "city" on bicycles, arrayed in "Prince Albert" coats.

The clothes of an American tourist still look funny to an

Englishman; how funny I never realised until I attended a play in London where an American was the object of good-natured caricature. He came on the stage with low shoes and silk shoe-laces, bright, thin socks, trousers held by a belt, no waistcoat, and jacket unbuttoned. The audience burst into roars of laughter and I laughed too, because he did look queer by contrast with the other actors. Then I suddenly realised that I was dressed precisely like the man they were laughing at!

One more reform must be made in men's dress; and I believe it will come. In very hot weather, men must be allowed to discard the jacket. Even a thin jacket, with its collar and shouldercloth, is intolerable. A clean, attractive shirt, with soft collar and necktie, and belt around the trousers, looks so sensible in hot weather that it ought to become the rule rather than the exception.

WOMEN

From "Adventures and Confessions" 1926

It is high time that some preacher showed a little chivalry;

Although women are necessary to the welfare, progress and success of the Church, and although they are tireless workers in Church and Sunday School and tireless listeners to tiresome preachers, they seldom receive compliments from the pulpit. On the contrary: women are more often preached *at* than praised. Paul, who knew less about women than about anything else, was the first Christian minister to make the vain attempt of putting "woman in her place"; and many modern pastors, with no more knowledge, and considerably less ability, have embarked on the same fruitless and perilous enterprise. Women have been denounced from the pulpit for their hair, their hats, and their gowns; a subject of which the only man qualified to speak is not a clergyman, but a tailor.

It is high time that some preacher showed a little chivalry; and I, an amateur instead of a professional, will now do so. Women who read this sermon will find something to their advantage.

I like the retort made by a woman novelist to a critic. He: "Most women have no sense of humour. " She: "Well, what of it? Most men have *no sense at all.*" If this be true, it might be historically accounted for by the child's version of what happened in the Garden of Eden. "God made Adam and he was very lonely, so God put him to sleep, took out his brains and made a woman."

"Hope not for mind in woman," said the poet Donne; but when he wrote that, he was not looking for mind.

If an honest man is the noblest work of God, a good woman is the finest.

Fashions change, manners change, the idea of beauty in anatomy, architecture, and in all the arts changes, but characteristics of the ideal man; modesty, amiability, gentleness have always characterised the ideal woman.

Clever young women who think the surest way to popularity is through shock, would do well to remember that the essentials of character are the same in all times and places. I remember, in a once famous farce called *A Trip to Chinatown*, a dialogue between a pretty girl whose facial charm was exceeded only by her audacity, and an unscrupulous man of the world. She asked him several questions: "You find me beautiful? fascinating? Brilliant? You like to be with me?" To all of which enquiries she received an emphatic affirmative reply. Then she asked, "And you would like to marry me, would't you?" "Not for gold or precious stones."

If an honest man is the noblest work of God, a good woman is the finest.

Women were just as necessary to the early church as they are now.

It is a rather curious fact that in the Old Testament the most famous women are villains, and in the New Testament the leading woman characters are saintly. I need only mention Jezebel and Delilah: Athaliah, more terrible than an army with banners; after these sinister persons, come Jael the murderer, and Deborah who glorified the cowardly deed; even the lovely and charming Ruth excelled chiefly in what is a second-rate virtue, obedience. But the New Testament women are immortal in their spiritual beauty. Mary the immaculate mother of Jesus; Mary Magdalene, the reformed harlot; Martha and her sister Mary, the first representatives respectively of low and high church; the woman of Samaria who spread the news of the living water; the sick woman who touched the hem of Christ's garment; the poor widow who contributed all her fortune and her heart with it; the woman who was content with crumbs from the Master's table; the woman who publicly blessed Christ's mother; the women who followed Him to the cross, *stayed there,* and were the first to visit the tomb.

In addition to these, the work of Peter and of Paul could not have been successful without the support of woman. Women were just as necessary to the early church as they are now.

It is often said that the interests of women are petty;

I do not understand why the fact that more women than men go to church should be regarded as counting against its value. The fact itself is more damaging to the men who stay away than it is to the church; but why should an assemblage of persons where women predominate connote intellectual inferiority? One minister complained to another that he could not get men to come to his services; and asked for his advice. The other said, “Why last Sunday I preached to an enormous audience composed entirely of men.” It was in the county jail.

The truth is that the proportionate worth of any undertaking is usually indicated by the excess of women over men who are interested in it. Firstclass music is surely not despicable; at orchestra concerts the women vastly outnumber the men. Art exhibitions are not for silly and stupid people; there are ten women to one man who show their interest by attendance. On the other hand, at a prize-fight the men still outnumber the women; and at a cock-fight I am informed there are scarcely any women at all, and those few disguised in men’s clothes; so that their presence and support will seem natural.

It is often said that the interests of women are petty; that they read in the newspapers only the Social Column and the

Fashion Page. Even if this is true, men's interests are hardly on a grander scale; for men will read with avidity five columns in fine print consisting of details connected with upper-cuts, left hooks, and side-stepping.

There is an instinct in women that leads them infallibly to choose and possess the best things in life.

It is just that women should support Christianity, for they owe their present independence more to Christianity than to anything else. Consider the position of women among Pagans, Mohammedans, American Indians, and heathen in general; and contrast that with their status in Christian countries. When Lafcadio Hearn lectured on English poetry to Japanese students at Tokio, he had considerable difficulty in explaining to them the conventional worshipful attitude maintained by English poets to women.

Women love religion, music, art, and poetry because they instinctively *know* that those things are immortal, whereas forms of government, politics, stock quotations, are ephemeral. Women do not have to be told that music and all forms of imperishable beauty are interesting; they *know* it. There is an instinct in women that leads them infallibly to choose and possess the best things in life.

Women do go forth to the scene of battle; but instead of going out to destroy, they go out to heal and restore.

If you wish to interest the average man in some enterprise, you must show him there is something in it making for his personal material advantage, or at all events for the practical welfare of the community; but the average woman will respond to an appeal based on beauty or nobility.

It used to be said by those opposed to granting political privileges to women, that in war they were anyhow inferior; for war was exclusively man's business. But since the days of Florence Nightingale – and even Lytton Strachey's adroit wit has not been able to darken her fame- we know that man has succeeded in making war the business of women. Women do go forth to the scene of battle; but instead of going out to destroy, they go out to heal and restore. The Red Cross, the Hospital Nurses, illustrate how women, by crucifying themselves, have saved men.

...**men and women must learn from each other.**

In *The Princess*, Tennyson, although old-fashioned and over conservative, was eternally right in insisting on the natural fact that woman and man are different. "Woman is not lesser man," but quite another thing. Thus the attempts of women to resemble men are as vain as they are silly. Why on earth should a woman want to be like a man? Yet Tennyson, in a few lines that should be read at every marriage-service, said that men and women must learn from each other.

Men should acquire sympathy and tenderness without losing virility; women should acquire understanding and the unprejudiced breadth of outlook that is born only of intelligence.

...let them think for themselves.

Women ought to cultivate their mental powers; much more than they do now. It is a true indictment against women that giving them the vote in national politics has produced no appreciable effect – which means that they have manifested no intellectual independence. There is no reason women should vote the same ticket as that voted by their husbands and fathers; let them think for themselves.

They have not, in the main, taken the privilege of the ballot seriously. They ought to qualify for citizenship by hard and faithful study of public questions. The League of Women Voters has done much; but there are more men today who can tell why they vote a certain ticket than there are women.

...the principle of development.

In his gossipy poem, *Old Pictures in Florence*, Browning makes a comparison between the perfection of Greek art and the imperfection of the human mind. He says that because Greek art is perfect, it reached its goal; it was finished; it therefore cannot develop. The human mind is faulty and clumsy, but it is *alive:* it has within its imperfections the principle of eternal development. Therefore when we look at perfect Greek statues, we should not repine because our bodies are so far short of the ideal human frame; we should rejoice, because with all our imperfections, nay because of our imperfections, our minds have something finer than any form of perfection – the principle of development.

...but every one can improve in mind and character.

Too many women are worried or despondent about minor matters, while they regard serious defect with complacency. It is of course important that they should look as well as possible, and dress as becomingly as their means will allow; but these are not the most serious considerations. Many women (and men) are keenly concerned about their looks and their clothes; am I looking my best tonight? are my clothes right? When really they should ask themselves, have I got any brains? and if not, how shall I supply this deficiency?

Every one, says Browning, looks at a perfect statue, and soliloquises, "Ah, I wish I looked like that!" a vain and impossible wish. It is difficult, by taking thought, that is, by worrying about it, to add a cubit to one's stature, or to change the curve of one's nose, or to acquire sudden wealth; but every one can improve in mind and character.

A heart whose love is innocent.

The Pope said of Pompilia that she was just as truly an angel living on earth, dressed in her street clothes, as she was in heaven, clad in radiant garments. Innocence in love, beauty of aspiration, cleanliness of heart, often increase facial beauty. Byron, who had had sufficient experience of light women, reserved his highest tribute for carefree innocence and noble impulses.

She walks in beauty, like the night
Of cloudless climes and starry skies,
And all that's best of dark and bright
Meets in her aspect and her eyes,
Thus mellow'd to that tender light
Which heaven to gaudy day denies.

One shade the more, one ray the less
Had half impair'd the nameless grace
Which waves in every raven tress
Or softly lightens o'er her face,
Where thoughts serenely sweet express
How pure, how dear their dwelling place.

And on that cheek and o'er that brow
So soft, so calm, yet eloquent,
The smiles that win, the tints that glow
But tell of days in goodness spent,-
A mind at peace with all below,
A heart whose love is innocent.

A perfect woman, nobly plann'd

Byron's great contemporary, Wordsworth, showed in one of his finest tributes to women that their attractiveness did not depend on romantic illusion; that with the right sort of wife and mother, daily intimacy did not lessen personal charm.

I hope that Hawthorne did not intend his character Hilda, in *The Marble Faun*, to be the ideal woman; for toward Hilda I cannot repress a feeling of aversion. "Her soul was like a star and dwelt apart"; but from the selfish sanctity of its seclusion, no real good resulted; no one was aided or comforted or inspired in the struggle of life. She was no help to sinners; she was their despair. She had the purity of an angel, but not the purity of a good woman. She was like one who should refuse to help a drowning man, for fear of soiling her clothes.

But Wordsworth showed that a good woman need not lose her ideality or her romantic, mysterious attraction, even in the daily household duties. She could be practical, sagacious, efficient; and yet have the fascination of a nymph in the moonlight.

She was a phantom of delight
When first she gleam'd upon my sight;
A lovely apparition, sent
To be a moment's ornament;
Her eyes as stars of twilight fair;
Like Twilight's, too, her dusky hair;
But all things else about her drawn
From May-time and the cheerful dawn;
A dancing shape, an image gay,
To haunt, to startle, and waylay.

I saw her upon nearer view,
A spirit, yet a woman too!
Her household motions light and free,
And steps of virgin-liberty;
A countenance in which did meet
Sweet records, promises as sweet;
A creature not too bright or good
For Human nature's daily food,
For transient sorrows, simple wiles,
Praise, blame, love, kisses, tears, and smiles.

And now I see with eye serene
The very pulse of the machine;
A being breathing thoughtful breath,
A traveller between life and death;
The reason firm, the temperate will,
Endurance, foresight, strength, and skill;
A perfect woman, nobly plann'd
To warm, to comfort, and command;
And yet a Spirit still, and bright
With something of an angel-light.

Little girls ... surpass boys in one important respect; their *ideals* are good.

There is no doubt that the average man has more physical strength than the average woman; it does not occur to any sensible woman to be ashamed of this inferiority. Well, history seems to show that in matters of initiative, in creative and administrative powers, the average man is again superior to the average woman. I cannot see why any woman should resent this any more than she resents her lack of physical strength.

For in the love of beauty, in ideality, in refinement, in purity, in accuracy of *feeling*, women are as superior to men as they are inferior in brute force. The best way to observe this is to consider children.

The instincts of the average healthy boy are mainly bad. Robbers and murderers are his heroes. In primary schools - not in college - the toughest boy is the idol of the others. I remember when I was six years old, there was in our room at school an absolute young villain, who would have destroyed the world, had he possessed sufficient power. He was vulgar, foul, pugnacious, cruel, and a bully; he was our hero. (He is now, I believe, in prison.) One day I was behaving badly, and some one said to me, "Why, if you go on in this way, you will be like Blank!" My eyes glowed with delight. He was my ideal!

The only way boys - who are savages at heart - become decent citizens and fit to live with - is through discipline, corporal punishment, public opinion, and the grace of God.

Little girls - very little - while they are not angelic, and may betray meanness and pettiness, surpass boys in one important respect; their *ideals* are good. They do not want to grow up and become adventuresses and scoundrels, they want to do good, help the sick and needy, stimulate the best impulses of men.

I happen to know the real value of the work done by women, and their sacrifices.

So many women have longed to be of use to men, have considered it their highest happiness to influence men in right directions, that the careers of many successful men have been accompanied by the sacrifice of women who could not bear to "stand in their way." I once saw a double-page picture in *Life*. It represented a vast space of deep water; a woman was drowning; all that was visible of her sinking body was her two hands above the surface; a few yards distant, a strong man was rapidly swimming *away from her;* and under the picture was the one word *Success.*

Many of our modern novelists love to expend their talents for ridicule and satire on evangelical churches, and especially on the organisations of women who do most of the work; the Ladies' Aid Society, the Foreign Mission Band, the Sewing Circle, and so on. Now three months of the year, I am associated with a small country church in a mid-western state (Huron City, Michigan). I happen to know the real value of the work done by women, and their sacrifices. In addition to the housework, they have to wash and dress the children, and from afar bring them to church and Sunday School; they do all this because they know the value of religion in daily life; they are not going to have their children brought up in ignorance and savagery.

I hope that in heaven God reserves an especially comfortable chair for the oldest daughter in a large family. This girl has no youth; from her earliest recollection she has always had to "mind the baby." She has to clean up after the younger ones, doing all the drudgery of a mother with none of the maternal passion that glorifies it.

Stabat Mater

Women not only have more passive courage than men, such as waiting in solitary anxiety, with none of the relief that action brings. They often have more of the desperate, reckless courage, that goes with the love of adventure. Marriage is an enterprise filled with more peril for a woman than for a man; a woman leaves the security of her home, and takes a chance with a stranger. No children would ever be born if men had to bear them; no man could stand the months of inactivity and sickness, with horrible agony and mortal danger as the climax. And if everything then turns out successfully, for three years the mother must know every instant in the twenty-four hours of every day, exactly where that child is. Are we men really worth all that agony and fatigue and boredom?

Well, there are some men who appreciate their mothers and their wives. They appreciate their mothers after the mothers are dead; and they appreciate their wives when they, the men, are sick.

The position of women as home-makers is also appreciated by some bachelors. The great Russian novelist, Turgenev, whom George Moore called the greatest artist since antiquity, said, "I would give up all my fame and all my art if there were one woman who cared whether or not I came home late to dinner."

The *Stabat Mater* applies not only to the mother of Jesus at the cross, it applies to millions of women who have "stood by" their husbands and their sons. The capacity of women to "stand by" can never be overestimated; that is why it is such an irreparable disaster for a man to lose his mother. A boy may be common-place, even stupid, the butt of his schoolfellows; but there is a woman at home in whose eyes he is a romantic hero; one who idealises him; one to whom he will never turn in vain.

www.ingramcontent.com/pod-product-compliance
Lightning Source LLC
Chambersburg PA
CBHW020424030726
47495CB00006B/1647